Common Cents

A common sense whole-of-life approach to taking control of your time and money

AF808202

By David Green

Common Cents

Common Cents

First Printed in Australia in 2005
International and eBook version published in 2015
This edition published in 2022
Written by David Green, Orange, Australia
www.dgreen.id.au
Photographs by Gwendolynn Green

National Library of Australia Cataloguing-in-Publication data:
Green, David, 1958- .
Common Cents : a common sense, whole-of-life approach to taking control of your time and money.
Includes index.
ISBN 0 9750412 1 5.
1. Finance, Personal. 2. Time management. I. Title.
332.024

Disclaimer

The author respects that each individual's circumstances are unique. He is neither a licensed financial adviser nor an accredited counsellor. This book is a personal account of his experiences and beliefs. The reader should seek professional advice before acting on its contents. By opening this book, the reader accepts this disclaimer and assumes full responsibility for his or her actions and their consequences.

About the author

David Green lives in Orange, Australia. He has been married for 38 years and is the father of an average Australian family of 2.4 children (boy, girl, dog [1]).

David holds a degree in Computer Science attained at the University of Melbourne, a Masters degree in Accounting from the University of New England, and is a Member of the Institute of Public Accountants in Australia.

For seven years, from 1995 to 2002, David wrote for *The Bush Telegraph* (a local newspaper in the Hornsby to Hawkesbury region of Sydney) a weekly column titled *Priceless Pearls*, in which he drew on life experiences, sports, movie themes, and current events, to inspire people and make them laugh. In 2003, David published his first book, titled *Toast*, which is the story of his family's experiences facing

[1] Sadly our beloved dog *Bronte* died in 2013, however I've left all references to her intact because these stories and pictures of her continue to inspire and make us laugh.

bushfires the previous year and coping with post-traumatic stress.

In this book, *Common Cents*, David draws on his experiences in financial management, project management, and family life. He worked in finance and project management for AGC and IBM for seventeen years, and spent eleven years as a self-employed accountant to small business. In the chapter titled *Down in the Dumps*, David draws on the negative experience of being unemployed and the simultaneously positive experience of being "Mr Mom" for three in-between years. Between 2007 and 2015 David managed the finances of two international charities. A tree-change in 2015 took him from Berowra to Orange, a cooler climate city four hours west of Sydney. Now the Greens turn blue in Orange.

David gives many unique, helpful and humorous insights into the twin worlds of time management and money management. With a *first things first* kind of attitude, he focuses on the *big picture,* or *big-ticket items* that will help the reader evoke *big change* in their life. Without this focus, he puns, the reader will be destined to *small change.*

David's vision is to see people taking control of their time and money, getting their priorities right and leading well-balanced lives. His writing style is direct and down-to-earth. He calls himself *"an ordinary bloke writing for ordinary people."*

Anyone will benefit from reading this uncommonly sensible book.

Why you *shouldn't* read this book

1. No time
2. No money

Why you *should* read this book

1. No time
2. No money

You're too busy *not* to read this book. You can't *afford* not to read this book.

Here's a story to illustrate my point:

Once upon a time, there was an army fighting a battle with single shot rifles, when an arms dealer arrived at field headquarters to demonstrate a new weapon. The commanding general refused to see the dealer because he was too busy fighting the battle. Besides, he couldn't afford new weapons. The ones he had still worked and he needed to save his money to fund the war for the next twelve months he expected it to last. *No time. No money.* Sound familiar?

The dealer left and went to the other side. The other general had no time and no money either. But he still took time out from the battle to look at the dealer's new weapon - a machine gun! He bought it and put it to use straight away. Initial losses on the other side were high but they quickly surrendered and the war was over in a week. Many lives were ultimately saved on both sides and both sides saved more than half their budgets because of the shortened campaign.

The moral of the story is this:

The first general couldn't see the wood for the trees. He had no time and no money and his response was to jealously guard what he had for fear of losing it.

As a result, he lost everything.

The second general had no time and no money either, but he saw a better way to invest the time and money he had.

As a result, he got more of both, not less.

Common Cents

It's just common sense, isn't it!

Contents

Table of Figures

Introduction

G'day and welcome to *Common Cents, a common sense approach to taking control of your time and money*. The title of the book is an obvious pun on the words *common sense*, which my dictionary defines as:

> **Common sense** *n.* **1.** good practical sense in everyday affairs. [Oxford]

That's exactly what I hope *Common Cents* will be for you - good practical sense in everyday affairs. Time and money affect every aspect of our lives, which is why I take a whole-of-life approach to writing about them. I hope you get some serious benefits while having a laugh or three with me along the way. You know, life has delightful ways of teaching its students its lessons. For instance, you'll find out that even watching a football match or a children's cartoon can help you save time and money.

I also hope *Common Cents* serves to confirm many things you already knew or suspected were true and to give you the skills and the confidence needed to put them into practice. That's why I came up with my own definition of common sense to complement the Oxford's:

> **Common sense** *n.* **2.** something you never realised you knew until someone told you. [Green]

Common Cents

This isn't a book full of theories; it's a book full of experiences taught to me by the school of hard knocks. Every word I write in this book is from personal experience of getting it wrong the first time and then learning what works. In hindsight, it all seems like so much common sense to me. The problem is that we're *all* like children, in that we learn much better by experience than by being told. My challenge to you is, ***break the mould!*** Don't be deluded. Learn from someone else's experience.

"The Book I would pass to my children would contain no sermons, no shoulds and oughts. Genuine love comes from knowledge, not from a sense of duty or guilt."
- Alan Watts (1915 - 1973), philosopher and author.

Now, here's a quick tour of the book. Chapters one and two introduce the *big picture* or *big-ticket items*, which will help you realise *big change* in your life. Without these, you'll be destined to *small change* (pun intended) for the rest of your life. Chapters three and four introduce day-to-day time and money management skills. Chapters five through eight describe what can go wrong to wreck the best-laid plans of mice and men, and more importantly how to overcome them. Chapter nine introduces a new way of thinking outside of the box and chapter ten introduces a six-step formula for decision-making, planning, and problem solving. The appendix contains a simple model for personal budgeting and cash flow management.

I hope you enjoy reading *Common Cents* as much as I enjoyed writing it.

David Green, March 2005

Common Cents

Chapter 1 - Getting your priorities right

Time and money - the two go hand in hand. As they say, time *is* money. Throughout this book, I'm going to introduce you to many common sense principles that you can use to take control of your time and money.

You might say there are four kinds of people in this world. There are those who have plenty of money but no time - typical of corporate executives for instance. Then there are those who have plenty of time but no money - the unemployed for instance. And then there are those with no time and no money - the majority of us! And finally there are those with plenty of time and plenty of money - the rich and famous.

My purpose isn't to teach you how to join the rich and famous, because that won't make you happy. Suicide is prevalent among the rich and famous too, you know. No degree of material prosperity will content you, because you'll always want more. My favourite way of expressing this is:

All I ever want is a little more than I'll ever get

No, my purpose is to *redefine* prosperity and show you how to prosper in *all* areas of your life. My definition of prosperity is:

Sufficiency in all things
and abundance in the best things [2]

For instance, you can only eat three meals a day and drive one car at a time. Fancy food and a flash car won't help you do those things any better, so you only need sufficiency in those things. On the other hand, you can never give too much time to your family and friends, so you need abundance in your relationships.

Common sense tells you how foolish it would be to put your priority on acquiring material wealth and spending it on bigger toys at the expense of your relationships with family and friends. Material wealth can be eaten or destroyed over time but relationships, if they are nurtured, can improve over time and become your most prized possessions. When you're in a hospital bed or a nursing home, your car won't come to your bedside to lift your spirit. If you've neglected your family or friends, they might come but their presence won't be uplifting. Good relationships are your most prized possessions.

---

[2] Inspired by 2nd Corinthians 9:8 *"that you, always having all sufficiency in all things, may have an abundance for every good work."*

Common Cents

If you haven't got your health, your life is going to shut down regardless of how well you're doing in every other aspect, so you need abundance in your health, too. Common sense tells you how foolish it would be to work long hours in a stressful job only to suffer a heart attack and die, or create a rift in your family that ends in alienation or divorce.

In his classic book, *A Christmas Carol*, Charles Dickens' character Ebenezer Scrooge was a wealthy but unhappy man who exploited his employees and looked down on the poor people around him. In a material sense, Scrooge was the richest person in the story. But in my eyes, and in the author's, he was the poorest. Scrooge was a poor, pitiful man whose material wealth didn't make him happy. The reason he was unhappy is that his priorities were all wrong.

You don't measure prosperity in common dollars and cents.

A prosperous life is a *whole* life that is in balance and bearing good fruit. You need to prosper in *all* areas of your life. To achieve that, you have to get your priorities right *now*.

PRIORITY NUMBER ONE

You need to invest time and money in your family relationships

If you don't, then at the very least *you'll* be miserable. At the worst, they'll look elsewhere - other people, TV, sex, drugs - for the love and comfort they need from you. And if divorce, sexually transmitted diseases or drugs cast their shadow on your doorstep, they'll cost you big time in both time and money. Neglecting your family in the pursuit of material wealth is false economy.

Take the example of a man who is rich in material wealth and bent on the pursuit of wealth and power in his business or his job. He's working long hours and weekends, and even when he *is* home he's still thinking and talking business and finance. He's doing it with the good intention of providing financial security and material comfort for his family. The problem is that his wife and children need his *time* even more than they need his *money*. He's working hard for his family but he's destroying his family in the process. He's becoming a stranger to them.

His wife married him to be her lover,
not her bank manager

She wants a divorce. His children are losing respect for him. As a result, they're losing respect for mum too. They're losing respect for their teachers at school. They're losing respect for all authority. They're becoming undisciplined and introverted. With the lack of parental guidance and involvement, they're bored, so they spend more time watching useless TV and video games. They're becoming bored with these too and they're turning to drugs and sex and violence for kicks.

By his efforts, this man is sabotaging everything he's working for. He's working for his family's future but destroying his family in the process. He's building a financial nest egg but when his wife divorces him and his kids disown him, he'll lose the money, along with his self-esteem and reason for living. This man's efforts will be in vain because his priorities are all wrong. He doesn't know the difference between a house and a home. Home is where the heart is. A house is just an empty building.

Better to live in a poor home than a rich house

It doesn't make sense, does it? Yet this is happening in families all around you. Maybe it's happening in your family. The cause isn't always overwork. Under-employment, for example, can lead to depression in a man or woman and result in the same kind of family breakdown.

People need people. Wives need their husbands and husbands need their wives. Children need their mum and they need their dad. That's been true since the beginning of time. Nothing has changed in human nature to negate that simple common sense truth.

Give them each at least a little bit of your undivided attention every day, and splash out at least once a month. Write it in your diary, or wherever you put reminders of important appointments.

Be prepared to give priority to unexpected interruptions, too, because the important things in *their* lives don't necessarily appear on your agenda or run to your timetable. Little things can make or break a relationship.

Earn their respect. Your word is your bond. Don't break your promises. Don't make promises you can't keep. If you say you'll be home at seven to read your daughter a bedtime story, be there at quarter to seven. Give them a *pleasant* surprise! Don't turn up at nine o'clock and expect nobody to care. If you make a business appointment and the person you're meeting turns up fifteen minutes late, you're really annoyed. Don't expect your family to put up with it any better than you do.

I've been married for over thirty years. In early years, I was a workaholic. I had a job that I liked and it paid well. We never had to think twice about buying anything we wanted. I thought I was doing the right thing, working hard and making a good living for my family. But my wife was desperately unhappy and that affected me. She wanted my time and attention more than money and the things it could buy. Her unhappiness was like a dripping tap. Like Chinese water torture, the individual drops have no discernible effect but continued application will drill a hole through your head.

Husbands, if you want a happy life, make your wife happy. It's a simple case of enlightened self-interest: if you make her happy, she'll love and respect you more, and then you'll be happier.

Wives, if you want a happy life, make your husband happy. It's a simple case of enlightened self-interest: if you make him happy, he'll love and respect you more, and then you'll be happier.

Don't wait for the other one to take the first step. Like in dancing, someone has to lead or you both go nowhere.

It takes two to tango but only one to take the first step

I have a son and a daughter. I'm horrified when I occasionally hear parents say they'll let their children make up their own minds and set their own values in life. *HELLO?* Every day, children are bombarded with directions, suggestions and values from their peers, from their teachers, from other adults and from the media - television, video and computer games, the Internet, magazines, etc. Undoubtedly, some of those influences are positive. Undoubtedly, some are not.

Dorothy Cohen, the US educator and child development specialist, wrote:

"Unfamiliar as yet with the full story of human response, they are being misled when they are offered perversion before they have fully learned what is sound." [3]

A child fully trained will be like his teacher [4]. Who's teaching *your* children?

If parents leave their children to make up their own minds, nothing of the sort will happen. What *will* happen is that *someone else* will influence their children and effectively make up their minds for them. That's what I call a family

---

[3] The Learning Child, *"Beyond the Home to School and Community"* (1972). Source: www.bartleby.com/66/3/12803

[4] Luke 6:40 *"everyone who is perfectly trained will be like his teacher."*

own-goal. It's just common sense, isn't it! If not, the advertising industry and free-to-air television *wouldn't even exist*, and yet they've thrived for more than half a century.

The younger children are, the easier they are to influence, for better or for worse. There's an old Jesuit maxim:

"Give me a child for the first seven years,
and you may do what you like with him afterwards." [5]

Muriel Spark, in her book, *The Prime of Miss Jean Brodie,* put it like this:

"Give me a girl at an impressionable age
and she is mine for life." [6]

I like to put it this way:

If they don't learn to heed me when they're toddlers,
they sure won't heed me when they're teenagers

A little investment of my time when they're young, and wanting me, will pay off big time when they grow up and have less need of me. Harry Chapin's song, *Cat's In The Cradle,* is a sobering reminder of this. It's so good, I've reproduced it here in full...

---

[5] *Lean's Collectanea* vol.3 (1903); found in: The Oxford Dictionary of Quotations, fifth edition, #647:16.
[6] www.bartleby.com/66/5/54905

CAT'S IN THE CRADLE

Words and Music by HARRY CHAPIN and SANDY CHAPIN

My child arrived just the other day,
He came to the world in the usual way.
But there were planes to catch, and bills to pay.
He learned to walk while I was away.
And he was talking 'fore I knew it, and as he grew,
He'd say, "I'm gonna be like you, dad.
You know I'm gonna be like you."

And the cat's in the cradle and the silver spoon,
Little boy blue and the man in the moon.
"When you coming home, dad?" "I don't know when,
But we'll get together then.
You know we'll have a good time then."

My son turned ten just the other day.
He said, "Thanks for the ball, dad, come on let's play.
Can you teach me to throw?" I said, "Not today,
I got a lot to do." He said, "That's ok."
And he walked away, but his smile never dimmed,
Said, "I'm gonna be like him, yeah.
You know I'm gonna be like him."

And the cat's in the cradle and the silver spoon,
Little boy blue and the man in the moon.
"When you coming home, dad?" "I don't know when,
But we'll get together then.
You know we'll have a good time then."

Well, he came from college just the other day,
So much like a man I just had to say,
"Son, I'm proud of you. Can you sit for a while?"
He shook his head, and he said with a smile,
"What I'd really like, dad, is to borrow the car keys.
See you later. Can I have them please?"
And the cat's in the cradle and the silver spoon,
Little boy blue and the man in the moon.

"When you coming home, son?" "I don't know when,
But we'll get together then, dad.
You know we'll have a good time then."

I've long since retired and my son's moved away.
I called him up just the other day.
I said, "I'd like to see you if you don't mind."
He said, "I'd love to, dad, if I could find the time.
You see, my new job's a hassle, and the kid's got the flu,
But it's sure nice talking to you, dad.
It's been sure nice talking to you."
And as I hung up the phone, it occurred to me,
He'd grown up just like me.
My boy was just like me.

And the cat's in the cradle and the silver spoon,
Little boy blue and the man in the moon.
"When you coming home, son?" "I don't know when,
But we'll get together then, dad.
You know we'll have a good time then."

On his "Verities and Balderdash" and "the Gold Medal Collection"
Source: www.harrychapin.com/music/cats.shtml

So, make it a priority to invest a little time in your family each day. Why not make it a habit to eat your evening meal together around the table, with the television turned off. Maybe turn on some music that everyone enjoys. Ask each member of the family, *"How was your day?"* Kids sometimes find that hard to answer, so then I try a few other tacks... *"What was the best thing about your day?"*... *"What was the worst thing?"*... *"What was* one *good thing?"* If you're sharing the morning meal, try *"What are you looking forward to the most, today?"* or *"What are you looking forward to the least, today?"* Lots of good sharing and helpful parenting can come from paying attention to the answers to those simple questions. Don't forget to answer those questions for yourself, in a positive and uplifting way.

In the Bruce Willis and Michelle Pfeiffer film, *The Story of Us,* they called this "Hi-Lo." At the evening meal, each family member was asked, in turn, *"What was your high today?"* and then *"What was your low?"*

Whenever possible, at least once a week, share something positive and uplifting that you've read or learned about during the week. Any team leader in a work or sports situation would do all these things and more to maintain communication and to build up a team. Think of your family as your home team.

Then, at least once a month, you need to give each member of your family some special individual attention and also do something special as a family together. Make it a priority.

PRIORITY NUMBER TWO

You need to invest time and money in friends

People need people. Human beings are social creatures. We need a shoulder to cry on at times, a listening ear, a word of encouragement, a helpful suggestion from an objective but friendly associate. You need friends away from your work and family and you also need them at work. A good team gives its members energy and inspiration. This applies at work, on the sporting field, and in other situations.

Without friends, you'll have no one to turn to when things get tough in your job, in your business, or in your marriage. You'll find it too easy to give in to the temptation to quit. A good friend can help you cope at those times and save you from making a bad decision you'll regret later on. Ignoring friends and being a loner is false economy. Make it a priority to invest time and money in building friendships.

The best way to have a friend is to be a friend

Some people who complain about not having friends actually push people away by their own complaining and expectations. They expect others to befriend them and to live up to their expectations.

It's popular these days for people to focus on their rights. That's fine to a point but it can go too far. Just imagine the logical extension of this push for rights... Eventually, we'll live in a world where *everybody* is sitting around waiting for *somebody* to give them their rights, but there'll be *nobody* left to take responsibility for *anybody*.

If we all take care of our *responsibilities* first, our *rights* will follow as a natural consequence.

Take the initiative to *be* a friend. Once a week, or once a month, invite someone round for lunch or dinner. Kill two birds with one stone: invite another family with children of similar ages to yours out for a picnic. That way, you'll be giving attention to two priorities at once - family *and* friends.

PRIORITY NUMBER THREE

You need to invest time and money in looking after your health

If you don't look after your health, you won't be able to enjoy your wealth. There's no point accumulating a great retirement fund if you die young or are too frail from neglecting your health to enjoy it.

I'm not a health expert, but to me there are three main aspects to good health:

Eat sensibly, exercise regularly, and drive carefully

Health tip number one: *We are what we eat*

My family has a pet dog, a Welsh Pembroke Corgi. The breeder told us what to feed her and what to avoid. The dog eats better than we do. We eat lots of things that we won't dare feed as scraps to the dog because of the breeder's warnings. We need to learn from that and feed ourselves more wisely.

Take *time* to select and prepare healthy food. In our busy lives, we get caught up in the time trap, rushing to work and meetings and so on and rushing our meals and grabbing fast food. Time is money and it's worth both time and money to you in the long run to take better care of your health. If you don't, you'll end up with medical problems that will cost you *big time*, in both time *and* money, to treat. Or you'll die young. Either way, taking shortcuts in healthy eating is false economy.

Healthy eating will save you money in the short term as well as the long term. Have a look in your shopping trolley this week. The desserts, confectionery, soft drinks and other unhealthy luxuries are the dearest items and can make up half your bill. Fast food is dearer still, and it certainly doesn't make financial sense to spend a day's wages at a restaurant when you could feed the family a healthy meal at home for a fraction of the cost.

Now, I'm not suggesting we all eat Brussels sprouts and drink water for every meal the rest of our lives. I'm just saying let's think about it and be a bit more sensible about our eating and drinking habits. Indulge your gastronomic lusts in moderation. It will pay dividends in the long run.

Also, eat more slowly and stop eating before you feel full. I've heard that hunger subsides after twenty minutes, no matter how much we eat.

I almost forgot to mention tobacco and alcohol, because they're so obvious. So I'll be brief: tobacco and alcohol are both expensive and unnecessary. Steer as far clear of them both as you can, for the sake of your health *and* your wealth and your family.

Health tip number two: *Use it or lose it*

Every part of your body needs regular, moderate use to remain in good condition. You can lose the use of parts of your body that you over-use or under-use in your work. Then you end up wasting time and money going to doctors and hospitals to rectify the problems.

I admit to a personal weakness in this area. I work at a desk, with a computer, most of the time. Everything I love to eat is bad for me and I find exercise boring. So my wife hides the chocolate around the house and I get exercise hunting for it.

Seriously, though, find a sport or an activity you enjoy and invest time and money into it.

For years I coached my son's soccer team. Now I do refereeing. My original motive in volunteering was to ensure my son and the rest of the team got outdoors and away from the idiot box at least a couple of times a week and got a bit of exercise and learnt a bit about teamwork and helping one another. A secondary benefit is that *I* get a bit of exercise too, running around the oval twice a week. So it's good for my family *and* my health.

I started going to the local gym, or fitness centre, twice a week. I find the supervision and the camaraderie both a help and a motivator. My trainer actually told me not to exercise hard between sessions. I love that kind of advice. The gym charges on a short-term basis, unlike some that demand an up-front payment of a year's membership. I wouldn't recommend that, because if you don't continue, or if they close down, you'll waste your money.

Health tip number three: *Be cool in the car*

Driving a car is probably the most costly and dangerous thing that most of us regularly do. That's why I single it out. If, by being a bit more careful, you avoid even a minor accident, then at the very least you'll save yourself a lot of time and money getting your vehicle repaired.

Treat the speed limit as an upper limit, not a lower one. Keep plenty of stopping distance between you and the vehicle in front. Pull over when you're tired. Better late than never. Don't drive if affected by drink or drugs. Don't phone or text, or program your GPS while driving; even hands-free, it's daft to think you can do that and still have your mind fully focused on the road, because you need to be alert and ready to respond in a split second to changes and dangers around you. The moment your attention is diluted or diverted ever so slightly, you lose that potentially life-saving edge. It's just common sense.

Another tip on driving: do it less often. If you can walk to your appointment, take the time to do so. You'll do your health a favour in more ways than one and you'll save money on fuel.

Finally, batch up your errands so you do them all in one trip instead of lots. That will save you time *and* money.

PRIORITY NUMBER FOUR

You need to invest time and money in a consuming interest, or hobby

Choose something that uses different muscles to your work. For instance, if you work behind a desk, find an interest standing up, like dancing or woodwork.

If you retire from the workforce without a consuming interest, you're going to be bored to death. Literally. Don't risk it.

You want to live long enough to get even with the taxman and your super fund, don't you?

Excess stress is not healthy, but neither is idleness. You need a consuming interest apart from your work to provide a safety valve. It will also be good for your health, which will have flow-on financial benefits. And it will give you something else to talk about and make you a more fun person for your family and friends to be with.

If you're unemployed, depression can get you down. Find a consuming interest and use your time to advantage. Read a good book. Join a service club or a sports club.

A *consuming interest* is one that you can't get enough of. It's an interest that lasts a lifetime. When you have a consuming interest, you're never bored.

My son loves music and my daughter loves animals. Those are good, healthy, consuming interests. So I've invested in them. I bought my son a guitar and guitar lessons and I bought my daughter a puppy. I continue to encourage and invest in their interests. Hopefully they'll never join the "I'm bored" crowd.

If you don't have a consuming interest, asking yourself these questions might help you find one:

What gets you really motivated?

When you're tired, what sparks action or interest in you?

What do you like to read about?

What is it, once you start talking about it, you can't stop?

What will get you up at three o'clock in the morning?

1. Make these four areas your priorities: **Family**, **Friends**, **Health** and **Hobbies**. Career and financial success will be to no avail unless you get these four right first. You can't put them off. These four can't wait.

2. You have to invest time and money to get them right. They're the big-ticket items that will save you time and money in the long run if you get them right now. If you want *big change* in your life, you've got to get the big picture right first. Otherwise, you'll be consigned to *small change* (pun intended) for the rest of your life.

Chapter 2 - Let it be written, let it be done

In Cecil B. DeMille's film production, *The Ten Commandments*, Yul Brynner plays the character of Pharaoh. Whenever Pharaoh makes a decision, he says, *"Let it be written, let it be done."* His scribe who follows him everywhere writes his words down and they are immediately enacted as law. I like that.

When you make a decision, or a plan, write it down. If you don't write it down, it will probably be forgotten. Unlike Pharaoh, I don't have a scribe to follow me around, so I always carry a pen and a single sheet of notepaper in my shirt pocket. I make a point of only wearing shirts with pockets, for this purpose. When I think of something I need to remember, I jot it down, or else I use the "Notes" program on my smartphone. If I don't do that, I can't possibly expect to remember it later. The other advantage is that once I write it down, my mind is clear, instead of being dogged all day trying to remember it. Albert Einstein possessed one of the most brilliant minds in history, yet even he refused to clutter it with unnecessary information. He kept it clear for the things he *needed* to think about. I once heard him quoted as saying he didn't remember his own phone number because he knew where to look it up when he needed it!

If you want to take control of your time and your money, you have to get your priorities right first. In chapter one, I introduced four priority areas of your life that you need to invest time and money into: Family, Friends, Health and Hobbies. In this chapter, I'll help you make it happen.

First, write down the four priority areas as headings on a blank page. You can use the worksheet (Worksheet 1) provided below.

Next, below each heading, make a list of the people or the things that are important to you in that area of your life.

Finally, below each heading, make a list of the things that are positive and another list of the things that are negative in that area of your life right now.

Figure 1 - **Worksheet 1: My Priorities**

	Family	**Friends**	**Health**	**Hobbies**
What's important to me in this area of my life				
What's positive in this area of my life				
What's negative in this area of my life				

Now that you've established your priorities, set some goals for yourself.

Write down the four priority areas as headings on another page. You can use Worksheet 2 below.

Below each heading, write down a goal that you'd like to achieve in that area of your life.

You might have multiple goals over multiple timeframes.

Have at least one goal under each heading that you can achieve over the next twelve months.

Figure 2 - **Worksheet 2: My Goals**

	Family	**Friends**	**Health**	**Hobbies**
My Goals				
Activities I can perform that will help me achieve my goals				

Try to set "SMART" goals. SMART stands for: Specific, Measurable, Achievable, Results-oriented and Time-driven. Look at the examples in the table (Table 1) below. Now take another look at the goals you just set. Are they SMART goals? Can you SMARTen them up?

Figure 3 - **Table 1: SMART Goals**

Non-specific goal: *Spend more time with my wife*	**SMART goal:** *Take my wife out once a month*
Immeasurable goal: *Be a better friend*	**SMART goal:** *Invite a family to lunch one Sunday a month*
Unachievable goal: *Be the best dad in the world*	**SMART goal:** *Read to my children once a week*
Goal that is not results-oriented (has no purpose in terms of your priorities): *Save $1000 this year*	**SMART goal:** *Save $1000 this year to buy a new saw-table for my carpentry hobby*
Goal that is not time-driven (has no deadline): *Run a five-minute mile*	**SMART goal:** *Run a five-minute mile by the end of this year*

Having a goal, however, isn't enough - you have to do something to achieve it. Make a list of activities that you can perform on a daily, weekly, or monthly basis that will result in you achieving your goal. You can use Worksheet 2 above to write your activities beneath your goals. Once you're finished, make a copy of your goals and activities worksheet and put it on display where you'll see it and be reminded every day.

Out of sight is out of mind

Keep your goals and your activity plan in plain view.

You've established your priorities, you've set your goals, and you've made a list of activities you can perform to achieve your goals. Now *do it!*

One more thing about priorities:

You need to be equally strong in all four areas

It's not good enough to be strong in just three, because one area of weakness will pull the others down. It's not good enough, for instance, to have a good family life, good friends and a good hobby or interest, if your health is failing, because as your health degrades, your ability to participate and succeed in the other three areas will also degrade. I'll illustrate with three analogies…

ANALOGY NUMBER ONE

The car

A four-cylinder car engine has to fire equally on all four cylinders. If one cylinder is misfiring, then no matter how well the other three are firing, the performance and ride of the whole vehicle is limited by the performance of the weakest cylinder. The only cure is to tune up or repair the weakest cylinder.

ANALOGY NUMBER TWO

The chain

A chain will always break at its weakest link. When it breaks, no matter how strong the other links are, the whole chain is useless unless the weakest link is repaired and strengthened.

ANALOGY NUMBER THREE

The wheel

Picture in your mind's eye a four-spoked wheel. Imagine each of the four spokes as representing one of the four priority areas of your life. Look at Diagram 1.

Figure 4 - **Diagram 1: Your wheel of life**

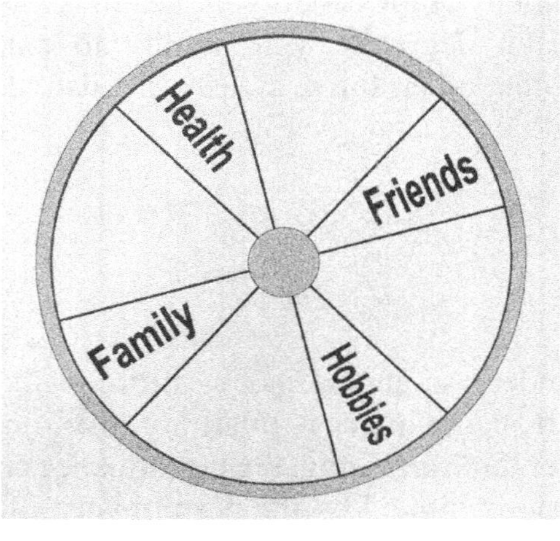

Imagine the four-spoked wheel in Diagram 1 attached to a monocycle frame, with a seat at the top. Imagine yourself riding atop that seat. If each of the four spokes is the same length and has the same strength, the wheel will rotate evenly and give you a smooth ride.

But if one spoke is shorter or weaker than the other three, you're going to get a bumpy ride and eventually the whole wheel will collapse. Look at Diagram 2.

Figure 5 - **Diagram 2: An unbalanced wheel gives a bumpy ride**

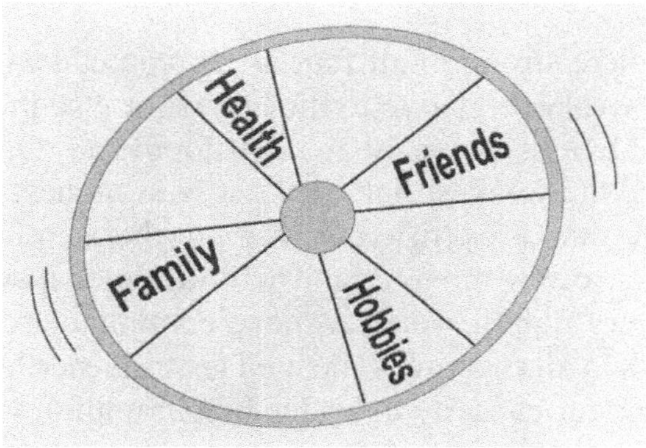

Let's take this analogy further...

A bigger wheel on a car gives a smoother ride because it will bridge potholes that a smaller wheel will drop into. You can apply this to your wheel of life: once the four spokes on your wheel of life are in balance, enlarge your wheel by setting new goals in each area. This will engage you in a continual cycle of balanced growth in each area of your life and it will increase your capacity to cope with bigger challenges or potholes in life, as you cross them.

ONCE A MONTH, GIVE YOURSELF A *WHEEL BALANCE*

Once a month, for each of the four priority areas of your life, ask yourself,

How am I doing?

Then ask yourself,

Which is The Weakest Link?

Even if you're strong in all four areas, you can still pick the one that's weakest relative to the others, or else the one with the most obvious potential for development. Once you've determined the weakest link, make it your highest priority to strengthen that area of your life in the coming month. Reaffirm or reset your goals and activities in that area. If you do this every month, you'll achieve continual strengthening and growth in all four areas. As you grow in each area, you're increasing your capacity to bridge bigger potholes in life!

If you find difficulty making a subjective judgement as to which is the weakest link, try a scoring system to rate your life in each of the four priority areas. When you've rated all four, the one with the lowest score is the weakest link demanding your attention. You can use the worksheet (Worksheet 3) provided.

You can extend and apply this method for continual improvement to your job or your business too.

Figure 6 - **Worksheet 3: How am I doing?**

	Family *Score 1 for Yes, 2 for Exceptional, 0 for No*	**Friends** *Score: 1 for Yes, 2 for Exceptional, 0 for No*	**Health** *Score: 1 for Yes, 2 for Exceptional, 0 for No*	**Hobbies** *Score: 1 for Yes, 2 for Exceptional, 0 for No*
Do I have a goal?				
Did I do anything this month to help me achieve my goal?				
Do I feel satisfied about this area of my life?				
Total scores:				

(The lowest score is The Weakest Link)

1. Write down your priorities
2. Set yourself SMART goals in each area
3. Do something about it
4. Check your progress regularly

Chapter 3 - Avoiding the ambushes

You know you need to invest time and money into the priority areas of your life. But you're busy already. And broke. Where are you going to find time or money to invest?

The easiest way to save time and money is to stop wasting them

Once you learn a few simple techniques for saving time and money, you can re-invest the savings into your priorities.

Think of it as taking money out of a cheque account and putting it into a term deposit. At present, your money is wasting away in a cheque account. Most of it you spend and the rest gets eaten away by bank fees. At the end of the day, you have less than when you started. If you put it into a term deposit, you can't spend it and it accumulates interest. At the end of the day, you'll have more than you put in. It pays dividends.

We don't *plan* to waste time or money. The wasters just take us by surprise. We get ambushed. But if we have a clear picture of what our priorities and goals are and fill our lives with priority-based activities, we run less risk of being ambushed by time-wasters and money-wasters.

Nevertheless, forewarned is forearmed. In a warfare situation, a small patrol of tired soldiers with poor weapons and no lookout is an easy target for an enemy ambush. Contrast this with a strong unit of fit soldiers bearing heavy artillery, with good reconnaissance and a good knowledge of the enemy's strengths, weaknesses and locations. This unit is unlikely to be taken by a surprise ambush and will be equipped to handle an attack if it comes. In the rest of this chapter, you'll learn how to become such a fighting unit in the war against waste. I'll expose a number of ambushes you're going to face and show you how to counterattack each one.

AMBUSH NUMBER ONE

Procrastination

Putting things off is a major time waster. Every time we put off doing something, it means we have to deal with it again later on.

The paper shuffle is a classic form of procrastination. You get a letter or a notice in the mail; you read it and leave it on your desk. Later on, you pick it up again, read it again and put it down, this time in your in-tray. The next day, when you're looking through your in-tray to see what you have to do that day, you come across the same piece of paper again. You read it again and replace it in your in-tray. So far you've read the same piece of paper three times and done nothing. You'll have to read it at least a fourth time before you deal with it.

A second form of procrastination is the *round tuit.* That's when you have a priority activity to do but you can never get a round tuit. That is, you can never get *around to it!*

Here are some tactics for avoiding procrastination…

TIME TACTIC NUMBER ONE

What's the best use of my time right now?

Fill your time with priority activities. If you have a spare fifteen minutes, do a little bit towards one of your priorities. Ring your spouse, talk to your kids, call a friend, or write the opening paragraph of that report you have to finish tomorrow.

TIME TACTIC NUMBER TWO

Start a "Do List"

This can be a desk diary, a wall calendar, or a pad of To Do lists. It doesn't matter what form it takes, as long as you look at it every day.

Personally, I prefer a desk diary. A calendar doesn't have enough space to write in and I can't carry it with me. A To Do list doesn't have sufficient structure to plan far enough ahead. I use an A5 sized desk diary, spiral-bound so it opens flat on the table, with a week to an opening - I find anything bigger is too bulky to carry around.

Use whatever works for you. If you prefer to use a simple To Do list, get a pad of them and write the days of the week atop the first seven pages. At the start of a new week, throw out the used pages and start again.

Make appointments with yourself to do your priority activities and write them in your diary, your calendar, or your To Do list. Break bigger projects up into bite-sized chunks and schedule them in. Use a soft pencil and an eraser, because priorities can change.

Don't let low-priority interruptions or procrastination keep you from your appointments.

To the left of each appointment, write a number and circle it. Next to activities that *must* be done that day, write and circle the number "1". Next to the others, write and circle the number "2".

Common Cents

Keep a separate page in your diary, on the back of your calendar, or the back page of your To Do list, for important things you need to do but don't have a specific timeframe for. Be careful though - if you want to get something done, you generally have to give it a timeframe or you'll never do it.

At the end of each day, transfer unfinished business forward to another day and cross off today.

TIME TACTIC NUMBER THREE

Open a "Do Drawer"

As soon as you make an appointment to *do* something and you write it down, put all the paper and other stuff related to it together in your Do Drawer. That way, it's out of sight and you won't fall into the trap of looking at it and studying it a dozen times before you actually need to deal with it.

If you have a lot of things on the go, your Do Drawer could be a drawer in a filing cabinet with an alphabetic index.

Another method is to set up a *tickler file*. This is a filing cabinet drawer with compartments labelled from 1 to 31. You file items under the number corresponding to the day of the month when you plan to deal with them.

TIME TACTIC NUMBER FOUR

Open a "Don't Drawer"

The Don't Drawer is where you put things that aren't a priority and aren't urgent either. Things you *don't* think you need but you're afraid to throw out. You put them in there so they're out of sight, but you can still find them if you need them. Be ruthless. If in doubt, chuck it out, or put it in the Don't Drawer.

Never look in the Don't Drawer - only open it to throw things in. Generally, the longer things stay there, the less important they become. If something *is* important, it will come back to you and you can fish it out.

When the Don't Drawer gets full, pull out the bottom half of the contents and put them straight into the rubbish bin without looking at them.

The Do Drawer is for things you *do* put in your diary. The Don't Drawer is for things you *don't* put in your diary.

TIME TACTIC NUMBER FIVE

Tell the truth

I don't like giving people bad news, such as a time delay on a project, a budget overrun, or a quality control problem. But putting it off only makes it worse in the long run for me and for everybody else.

Holding back the truth is the same as lying, because in the absence of bad news, everyone assumes by your silence that things are going ok.

When you start to lie, you have to keep lying to cover up the first lie. Pretty soon, as you weave an increasingly complex web of subterfuge, little white lies snowball into big whoppers. In fact,

There are no white lies,
only black ones

It was the Scottish novelist, poet, historian and biographer Sir Walter Scott (1771-1832) who first wrote,

"Oh what a tangled web we weave,
When first we practise to deceive!" [7]

Tell the truth tactfully, respectfully, openly and quickly.

If someone gives *you* bad news, don't shoot the messenger. Instead, be grateful that they were willing to *risk* telling you the truth. If you abuse people for giving you bad news, you discourage openness and honesty and create a culture of

[7] www.bartleby.com/100/338.25

subterfuge and politics. As a result, people start spending more and more of their time watching their step and covering their back instead of looking up and moving forward. Unfortunately, I see this happening all the time in business, in government, in fact all kinds of organisations. No organisation, where two or more people are gathered, is exempt from the risk of it. What a waste of time and money it is. One of my dearest wishes is to reform our political and legal systems that, by their adversarial nature, discourage truth, openness, and common sense.

If someone gives *you* bad news, listen. Beware of the condition known as *itching ears* [8]. When you have itching ears, you hear only what you want to hear. You ignore advice from people who tell you what you don't want to hear and you listen intently to people who tell you what you do want to hear. When you have itching ears, you reward people who tell you what you want to hear and you abuse and punish people who tell you what you don't want to hear. You drive away people who want to help you with the truth and you draw to yourself people who are willing to lie to you so they'll look good and benefit from your favour. When you have itching ears, you're a sitting duck for liars and con men. Remember this:

The sharp words of a friend are kinder
than the sweet whispers of an enemy [9]

---

[8] From 2nd Timothy 4:2-4 *"according to their own desires, because they have itching ears, they will heap up for themselves teachers, and they will turn their ears away from the truth, and be turned aside to fables."*

[9] Proverbs 27:6 *"Faithful are the wounds of a friend; but the kisses of an enemy are deceitful."*

Common Cents

If you're in business, you should reward customers who make a complaint (I mean the genuinely concerned customers, not the habitual whingers). How else will you know you have a problem? Think of it as cheap market research. For every customer that takes the time to complain, you can bet there are ten others with the same problem who didn't bother to tell you.

AMBUSH NUMBER TWO

Electronic entertainment media

Television, video, computer games and the like are expensive time wasters. We can all benefit from a bit of time-out, but we almost always overdo it when we turn these machines on. They draw you in and suck up your time.

They entertain you but they don't replenish you. When you finish, instead of being refreshed you feel more tired than when you started. A better use of your leisure time is to spend it on your interests or hobbies.

They're anti-social. They demand your full attention. They teach anti-social behaviour and values and they withdraw you from family and friends. When you finish, you're physically and emotionally drained.

They're bad for your health because you're sitting down and using the same muscles for hours on end. That's why plane travel is so tiring. Television strains your eyes and neck muscles and the interactive forms - video and computer games - also strain your back, arms and hands. When I was twenty-six, I contracted RSI from computer keyboard over-use. Today, kids of ten are getting similar problems.

Electronic entertainment media can short-circuit all four priority areas of your life - family, friends, health and hobbies. But they needn't. Here are some strategies for managing the electronic entertainment media in your home…

MEDIA STRATEGY NUMBER ONE

Is this uplifting?

Be selective about what you and your family watch. Remember the Jesuit maxim, *"Give me a child for the first seven years, and you may do what you like with him afterwards."* Extending that principle, up to the age of about ten I wouldn't let my children watch any television or videos that encouraged negative behaviour or attitudes. That has paid huge dividends in my family. My children have now learnt to self-censor what they watch.

You need to watch what your children are watching to judge its suitability. Not just for obvious things like coarse language, sex and violence. Think of it as enemy propaganda. Sometimes propaganda is obvious and odious but sometimes it's subtle and sweet. Lots of kids' shows with innocuous-sounding titles and cute-looking characters teach disrespect for parents and other authority. I think that watching a cute little cartoon koala bear called *Blinky Bill* being disrespectful to his parents does kids more harm than watching *Wylie Coyote* try to belt the living daylights out of the *Road Runner*. Though both are cartoons, Blinky Bill is more realistic, relatable and easily copied, viz: *"I'm Blinky Bill, I do what I will; I'm almost on my best behaviour nearly every day."* Wylie Coyote is unrealistic (a coyote on hind legs that purchases dynamite sticks by mail order?), unrelatable (ditto) and his actions and contraptions are impossible to imitate.

Many television shows today portray fathers as stupid and insensitive; they portray mothers as the caring and sensitive victims of dad's shortcomings, and they portray kids as smart and heroic. This is sweet and subtle propaganda that teaches kids disrespect and rebellion. To counter this, I don't suggest banning everything. I don't. But I vet what my kids watch and we talk about it. I correct any wrong messages they're seeing or hearing. I make sure they understand and learn to discern for themselves between right and wrong. Parents have to strike a balance between protecting their kids from enemy ambush and preparing them to fight it.

MEDIA STRATEGY NUMBER TWO

Ration their use

Limit each family member to, say, ten hours a week of all electronic entertainment. Be specific - name the shows they can watch and the games they can play. Help them plan the rest of their leisure time around their hobbies and interests.

MEDIA STRATEGY NUMBER THREE

Provide alternatives

A consuming interest is the best alternative.

If you fill your life with priority activities, you'll find you don't have time to waste on too many television shows and computer games. Encourage reading as an alternative to watching. Find books or magazines about your hobbies and interests. Play card games or board games occasionally as a family. Encourage sporting interests.

In the pre-industrial age, families worked and played together. Sons and daughters learned practical skills by helping their mums and dads in the home and out in the yard. I'm not being nostalgic or naïve; those times had their own hardships that we wouldn't wish to endure again. We can't go back to the past but we *can* learn from it.

AMBUSH NUMBER THREE

Impulse

Impulse buying, making unplanned and unnecessary purchases, is a major money waster. Impulsive activity is a major time waster. Things that take us by surprise often seem more urgent and more important than they really are. Here are some rules of thumb that you can follow to help you overcome the impulses…

IMPULSE RULE NUMBER ONE

Take a priority check

When you're tempted to spend time on an unplanned and non-essential activity, ask yourself, "*Is this a priority use of my time? Will this activity help me achieve one of my priority goals?*"

If the answer is No, don't do it.

When you're tempted to make an unplanned and non-essential purchase, ask yourself, "*Is this expense a priority? Will spending this money help me achieve one of my priority goals?*"

If the answer is No, don't do it.

IMPULSE RULE NUMBER TWO

Cool off

Let's say you've taken a priority check and your answer is, *"Yes, even though I hadn't planned it, this lines up with my priorities and my goals."*

Don't rush into it. Cool your heels. Since you hadn't planned it, it probably isn't that urgent. Talk to your spouse and anyone else it may affect. Make a list of the pros and cons. If you all agree it's a good idea, write down your decision and the reasons for it. Put it aside for a day, a week or a month, depending on the size of the investment. Write a note in your Do List to review the decision on an appointed day and put all the details in your Do Drawer, out of sight and out of mind until then.

A cooling off period like this will save you from making impulsive decisions in the heat of the moment that you'll regret later on. Priorities can change and other things can crop up in that time, too.

When the cooling off period has elapsed, revisit your decision. If everyone's still positive, go ahead with it.

IMPULSE RULE NUMBER THREE

There are no free lunches

Don't be fooled or tempted by "free gifts." Always remember these basic and well-known bits of common sense advice:

Everything has to be paid for

You get what you pay for

Risk is proportional to reward

Stick with who you know and trust

I remember years ago taking up an offer of free dance lessons. I enjoyed the lessons, so I paid for some follow-on lessons. Later, I learned that I paid more for the lessons I bought than students did who walked in off the street. I had paid an "advertising premium" on my lessons to compensate the dance studio for my "free" introductory lessons. There are no free lunches.

If you or your business evades or avoids paying taxes, the government doesn't close roads and hospitals. It simply shifts more of the tax burden onto those who can do least about it - ordinary wage and salary earners. If people make excessive insurance claims, insurance companies increase premiums to pay for the extra claims. Someone has to pay. There are no free lunches. So don't be fooled if someone offers you one.

Don't be fooled or tempted, either, by clever schemes or arrangements that promise you a shortcut to riches. They're gambles. All forms of gambling are designed so that most of the players lose. They have to be, otherwise their operators wouldn't make a profit and they wouldn't be in business to make the offer in the first place.

So here's what to do when you're offered a "free lunch": say *"No!"* quickly and forcefully. Say, *"No thank you, I'm not interested."* Don't listen to the sales pitch or you'll be sucked in. Use the cooling off rule as an escape.

Steer clear of limited offers, like "ten per cent off if you sign today." That's a dead giveaway that the promoter is sure you'll say no if you have time to think about it and make a rational decision. If the promoter is so sure it's a bad deal for you, why would you say yes?

Don't be drawn in by sales or specials. If you're planning to buy something anyway, you can wait for a sale to buy it. But don't buy something *because* it's on sale. Don't save ten percent to waste ninety per cent. Don't go - it's a waste of time and money. Did you hear the joke about the New Year's resolution? The character in the story makes a New Year's resolution to save money, and then plans to go to every store sale in the next twelve months to save as much as they possibly can!

IMPULSE RULE NUMBER FOUR

Empty pockets

Money in my pocket disappears, because it's too easy to spend on impulse. I never carry money in my pocket unless I have a specific purpose for it and plan to use it the same day. Even then, I carry only as much as I need.

I prefer not to use EFTPOS to get cash out of the bank or to pay for groceries either, because it's too easy to spend over my budget.

Once a week, I sit down for five minutes, look ahead in my diary and write a list of all the things I'll need cash for. I have a standard list of amounts I need *every* week, such as a budgeted amount for groceries, gym money, and a small amount of pocket money.

Then, once a week, I go to the bank or ATM and withdraw exactly the amount of cash I need for the next seven days. As soon as I come home, I put the cash into envelopes and write on them what they're for. I leave the cash in the envelopes and the envelopes in a drawer until I need them. This avoids the risk of spending the money on unplanned and unbudgeted things before the planned and budgeted things come around.

IMPULSE RULE NUMBER FIVE

Spread your money like butter

When I have the option of paying for some recurring expense, such as an insurance premium, in a lump sum or pay-by-the-month, I usually opt for pay-by-the-month. I do this to avoid the shock of getting a big bill every twelve months. If I pay in a lump sum, I might not have the money ready when the next annual bill arrives. Paying by the month ensures that I don't overspend on other things and then end up short when the next big annual bill comes due.

For the same reasons, when I have the option of paying an account such as my telephone bill quarterly or monthly, I always opt for monthly.

Some companies add a surcharge for the privilege of paying as you go. Even so, the significant benefits you'll gain outweigh the small price you'll pay.

I also avoid bulk buying. The reason is that you tend to use what you've got. Buying in bulk usually means your consumption rate increases, so you don't save in the long run. On the other hand, you might never use all you purchase. Either way, bulk buying is a gamble. My advice is to pay as you go, unless you're absolutely sure you won't waste it.

This rule applies only to recurring expenses. I don't apply it to one-off purchases. Quite the opposite. If I have the money, I'm best to pay it in full straight away, otherwise I risk spending it on other things and being unable to meet the payments when they fall due.

IMPULSE RULE NUMBER SIX

Credit control

Credit cards make great slaves and lousy masters.

Credit cards are a tremendous convenience. They save you having to carry lots of money in your pocket all the time for emergencies. And we all know what happens to money in your pocket - it disappears. Another advantage of credit cards is the monthly statement that helps you see where your money goes and provides a record for tax purposes.

On the other hand, credit cards are the *best friends* of impulse buying. For this reason, it's doubly important to apply the first three rules of impulse buying when tempted to use your credit card for an unplanned purchase. Remember the first three rules:

(1) Take a priority check,
(2) Cool off, and
(3) There are no free lunches.

If you can't control your impulses, cut up your credit cards. You'll save a LOT of money.

BEATING PROCRASTINATION

What's the best use of my time right now?

Keep a diary, a calendar or a To Do list
and fill it with priority activities

Open a Do Drawer

Open a Don't Drawer

Tell the truth

CONTROLLING ELECTRONIC ENTERTAINMENT
IN THE HOME

Is this uplifting?

Ration it

Provide alternatives

CONTROLLING YOUR IMPULSES

Apply a priority check to every activity and expense

Allow yourself a cooling off period

Common Cents

There are no free lunches
Empty pockets
Spread your money like butter
If you can't control your impulses cut up your credit cards

Chapter 4 - Parkinson's Laws

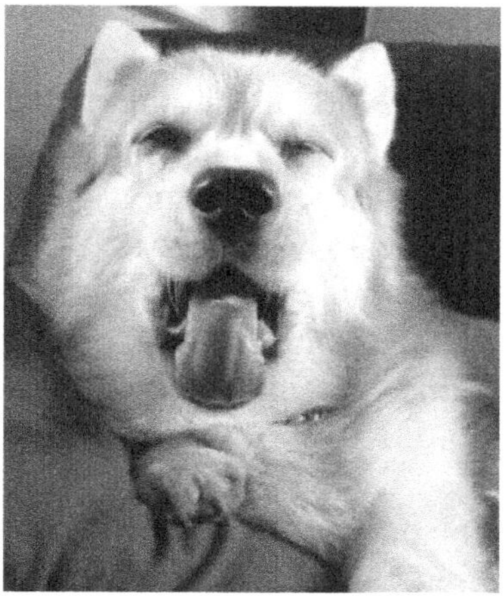

By now, you're starting to take control of your time and your money. You're getting your priorities right and learning to avoid the ambushes that have been robbing you up until now. Now you're ready to confront Public Enemy Number One in the war on waste – Parkinson's Laws!

Parkinson's Law is a classic truth taught in all time management classes. It was penned by the British historian and political scientist, C. Northcote Parkinson (1909-1993). It goes like this [10]:

WORK EXPANDS
TO CONSUME
THE AVAILABLE TIME

[10] The exact quote is *"Work expands so as to fill the time available for its completion."* Source: www.bartleby.com/66/29/43629

I'll illustrate by way of example…

Let's say I have a report to write which should take me about a day to complete. Now, if I allocate *two* days to finish the report, and have nothing else of equal or higher priority to do, I'll probably spend the whole two days getting it done. I'll spend the extra time pontificating and procrastinating over unnecessary details and adding extra tables and charts that make the report twice as long as it needs to be and cloud the issues in the process. I'll play with fancy spreadsheets to refine the figures to the last cent and make pretty coloured charts. In short, the report will be *over-cooked.*

The one-day version would be more concise and to-the-point. It would be more effective for its intended purpose, as well as a more effective use of my time. If I have two days available, I'd be better to finish the report the first day and take my family on a picnic for the second day.

Now, let's say I only have two hours to do the report. The result will be rushed, incomplete and full of errors. It will be *under-done.*

Having too much time on your hands is a curse but too little is no good either.

The point is that most activities have an optimum time frame.

Just in time

If you want to manage your time well, you have to learn to practise *just-in-time* time management.

Don't leave yourself too little time to do the job, and don't leave yourself too long either.

Just in time is a term coined by manufacturing and distribution industries. *Just in time* inventory management was invented out of necessity because inventory storage and management is a very costly business. If a manufacturer has goods sitting in warehouses or in yards doing nothing, they're costing him money. Warehouses and yards cost money to buy and maintain; the people who manage them have to be paid wages; and the money spent manufacturing the goods isn't recouped until the goods get into customers' hands.

To reduce these costs, manufacturers make their forecasting, ordering, manufacturing and delivery processes more efficient, so they have less inventory sitting in yards and warehouses doing nothing and costing them money. Then they need smaller warehouses or yards, fewer people to manage them and shorter lead times between the manufacture of goods and the receipt of payment for those goods.

The old way was to manufacture goods in *plenty of time* for when the customers want them.

The new way is to manufacture goods *just in time* for when the customers want them. Not too soon and not too late. Just in time.
Here's an example of how you can put *just-in-time* time management into practise yourself…

Let's say you have a job to do by 5pm tomorrow and you estimate it will take two hours to complete. Now, grab your diary, the calendar on the fridge, or whatever it is you use to remind yourself of important appointments. Make an appointment with yourself between 2pm and 4pm tomorrow to do that job. Don't give yourself too much time but don't put yourself under excessive pressure either. End of example.

Another good reason to schedule tasks just ahead of their deadline is that priorities and requirements can change.

Things that seem important and urgent today may be neither important nor urgent tomorrow. If you respond to every impulse instantly, you can end up wasting time on a lot of wild goose chases. Also, more information can come to light closer to the deadline that will help you do the task more efficiently.

The risk with *just in time* is that last-minute interruptions and emergencies, and unforeseen complications, can ruin your plans.
If the job is really critical, do it ahead of schedule if you must but still budget your time. Write it in your diary with a start and a finish time and stick to both.

So much for Parkinson's Law of Time Management. Next up is another universal law I've discovered which relates to *money*. I call it Parkinson's Law of Money Management, because although Parkinson didn't write it, it's based on his original Law. Parkinson's Law of Money Management is:

**EXPENDITURE EXPANDS
TO CONSUME
THE AVAILABLE INCOME**

In other words, we spend what we have. We live within our means. We never have enough. No matter how much we have, we always long for that one extra thing that's beyond our reach. As far as money is concerned, our attitude is…

All I ever want is a little more than I'll ever get

Over the years, my income has fluctuated wildly as I've moved from job to job and role to role. Throughout that time, I've found one constant in my life: No money in the bank! I spend it. Each time I have a change in fortune, I automatically adjust my lifestyle and my desires to suit.

Leaving money just lying there, doing nothing, is a sure-fire way to lose it. You're a creative person. You'll think of a way to spend it.

The only way to save money is to *hide* it from *you.*

Pay yourself

You can think of it as paying yourself. You're forever forking out money to other people; why not pay some to yourself!

So, how much should you hide? How much should you pay yourself?

When you're exercising, you have to stretch your muscles for them to grow. If you over-stretch, you risk tearing a muscle. If you under-stretch, you achieve nothing.

The same principles apply to your savings. You have to set yourself stretch goals to save. Don't be over-ambitious, or you'll fail and give up. Don't be under-ambitious either - you'll be surprised at how well you cope with less.

No matter what your income is, try hiding ten percent. If that seems too much of a stretch, start with less and work up to it. If you're applying all the principles learned so far in this book, you've got to be saving. It's important to hide those savings so you don't waste them.

Hide your money as soon as you get paid. The longer you leave your money idle, the more likely you'll consume it.

Ideally, take your savings straight out of your income. If you're a wage earner, your employer might have a facility to deduct a fixed amount or percentage from each pay and deposit it in a separate account. If not, use phone banking or Internet banking to transfer your savings to your hiding place as soon as you get it. You may pay a little extra in bank fees but the savings gained will outdo the costs incurred.

If you run a business, every time you receive money, transfer an appropriate percentage into a separate account for tax and other liabilities and transfer a percentage into another account for savings goals and rainy days (unplanned contingencies).

Whenever your income rises or your expenses fall for any reason, add the difference to your savings immediately. If you don't act sharply, you'll quickly consume the difference and forever wonder how you ever did without it, because *expenditure expands to consume the available income.*

When you finish paying off a debt, add the debt repayments to your savings immediately. You've been living without that money for the term of the debt, so you can keep on living without it. The difference is, up until now you've been paying that money to someone else. Now you can start paying it to yourself!

I don't mean for you to become a Scrooge, saving every last cent. Everything I've shared up to this point has been against that in principle. The point of this chapter is to show you how to save time and money so you have more of both to spend on your priorities. In any event, you should always plan to save a minimum of ten percent of your income.

The hiding place

Once you've decided how much to hide, the next thing to decide is *where* to hide it.

Some of you are probably thinking that under the bed is a good investment these days, with bank fees exceeding interest income (unless you have a *lot* of money). So, why *not* put it under the bed? The risk of hiding it under the bed is theft. If you hide it under the bed, the risk is you *might* get robbed. But if you put it in the bank, you *will* get robbed. The *bank* will rob you with its high fees and low interest.

Seriously, though, the problem with under the bed is that the main threat of robbery comes *not* from the occasional masked intruder. The main threat of robbery comes from *you. That's* why you have to hide it from yourself. If it's under the bed, or in your wallet for that matter, it's too easy for you to get at. It won't last *there* for long.

No, the answer to the question of where to hide it depends on your savings goals.

Your goal may be to reinvest your savings straight away into one or more of your priority areas - something for your family, friends, health or hobbies.

Debt first, ask questions later

I said earlier that we tend to live within our means. Actually, most of us live beyond our means, by the grace of debt.

If you have any debt, such as a mortgage or credit card, your first goal, after looking after your four main life priorities, should be to eliminate that debt. Put your savings into increased debt repayments.

If you have more than one debt, pay off the one with the highest interest rate first.

Debt is a noose around your neck. Apart from buying a house, I suggest you avoid it altogether.

Typically, people borrow money in good times. And they borrow as much as they can get approval for. The problem is, when harder times come, for instance through retrenchment or interest rate rises, they can't afford to keep up the repayments and sometimes have to sell their assets at a loss to get out of debt.

If you *are* planning to borrow money for something, try to get a flexible loan so you can vary the repayments, up or down, to suit your fluid financial position.
So much for debt.

If you don't have any debt, your goal may be to save for some special purchase, such as a family holiday, a car or a home renovation.

You may wish to put money aside regularly for Christmas, that time of year when all budgets go out the window.

It's wise to put money aside in a *rainy day* account for unexpected major expenses, like when the fridge and the washing machine both die in the same week and have to be replaced.

Under lock and key (your financial chastity belt)

I can't save money by leaving it in my everyday spending account. Or under the bed. To save money for a special project, for Christmas, or for a rainy day, I have to force myself to save by hiding some of my income from myself in a separate bank account. Preferably an account that's locked away so I can't withdraw from it on impulse.

I never withdraw funds from this account except under special circumstances…

The cooling off period

Firstly, I ask myself whether the withdrawal is for the purpose I put the money aside.

If it's not, I don't touch the money.

If it is, I still don't rush into it. I cool my heels. I've been saving for a long time and I don't want to waste it with an impulsive decision. I've been waiting this long, so a little while longer won't hurt.

I talk to my wife and to anyone else the decision may affect. We make a list of the pros and cons.

If they agree it's a good idea, I write it down, and I write down the reasons for it.

Then I put it aside for a day, a week or a month, depending on the size of the investment.

I write a note in my diary to review the decision on an appointed day and put all the details in my Do Drawer, out of sight and out of mind until then.
A cooling off period like this will save you from making impulsive decisions in the heat of the moment that you'll regret later on. Priorities can change and other, more important things can crop up in that time, too.

When the cooling off period ends, revisit your decision. If everyone's still positive, go ahead with it.

Excuses, excuses

Finally, stop telling yourself *"I can't afford it"* or *"I'm too busy."* When it comes to your life's priorities, those are lies. We're very resourceful when it comes to finding time and money to spend on things we want badly enough. I know people who one minute say they can't afford to put food on the table and the next minute they're buying a new car. I know people who can never find fifteen minutes to read their child a bedtime story but will get up at three o'clock in the morning to go fishing, or play eighteen holes of golf every weekend.

The acid test

If you're really not going to do something, don't say, *"I can't afford it"* or *"I'm too busy."* People will see you spend time and money on other things and they'll think you're a liar or a hypocrite. If you're really not going to do something, a more honest statement to make would be:

"It's not a priority"

Tell yourself *that,* the next time you start to say *"I can't afford it"* or *"I'm too busy."* Use it as a *litmus test* to see if your priorities really are right.

1. WORK EXPANDS TO CONSUME THE AVAILABLE TIME

   Practise *just-in-time* time management

2. EXPENDITURE EXPANDS TO CONSUME THE AVAILABLE INCOME

   - Pay yourself first
     - Find a good hiding place
     - Save ten percent of your income
     - Lock it up

   - Debt first, ask questions later
     - Reinvest it in your priorities, put it to retiring debt, or put it in a separate account for special projects and rainy days

   - Apply a cooling off period to withdrawals

   - Use the acid test to see if your priorities are right

Chapter 5 - Kicking an own goal

When I was coaching, I taught my soccer team that the objects of the game are to have fun and score goals.

If they're having fun, they'll put more effort into training, they'll put more energy and enthusiasm into the game, and as a result they'll score more goals. If they score more goals, they'll have more fun. The two go hand in hand. But if they focus on just one of the objects and ignore the other, it won't work.

For example, if all the focus is on just having fun, they'll run riot at training, they won't listen to instruction, and they won't play well on match day. As a result, they won't score goals, they'll lose every match, and that won't be fun for them.

If they focus solely on having fun, they won't get any*!*

On the other hand, if all the focus is on scoring goals and winning matches, the coach and the players will get too serious, they'll start worrying over results, they'll start abusing each other for mistakes and they'll get depressed when they make an error themselves. They'll stop having fun, and pretty soon, they won't want to play. If they don't play, they don't score goals.

If they focus solely on scoring goals, they won't get any*!*

It's all about getting the right balance.

Whenever I think about balance, I think of a pendulum.

A pendulum swings from extreme left to extreme right and back, continuously. The only *steady* state, the only state a pendulum can remain in for more than a moment, is in the centre, the point of balance or rest.

Look at the pendulum in the following Diagram 3.

Figure 7 - **Diagram 3: The pendulum swings of life**

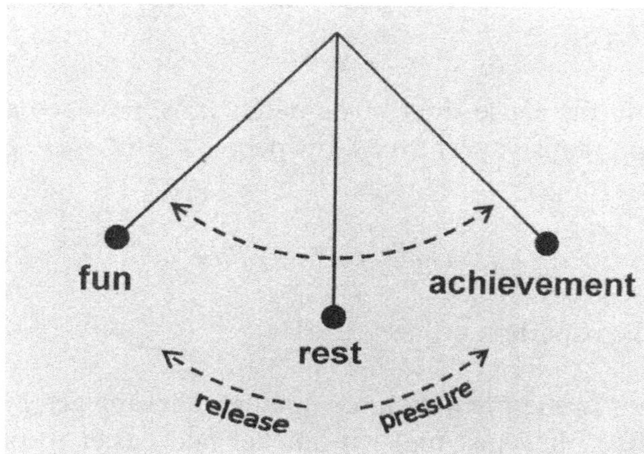

The extreme left of the arc of swing is labelled *fun* and the extreme right is labelled *achievement*. The centre is labelled *rest*. Movement of the pendulum from left to right is labelled *pressure* and right to left is labelled *release*.

Like a motionless pendulum, you can try to live your life forever in the central steady state of *rest*. That might sound appealing but it's the way to an early grave. Like the pendulum, you need variety and movement.

Future shock

Around the 1970's, emerging computer technology prompted a euphoric view of the future, based on the futurists' prediction that by the end of the century computers would replace a lot of tedious office and process work.

In this idealistic future, people would work fewer hours and have more leisure time to do what they like. Electronic communication would replace letters, memos and reports. Thus arose the twin myths of the leisure society and the paperless office.

They got the cause right. Computers *have* replaced a lot of work previously performed by people. But they got the effects wrong.

The paperless office

First, the paperless office…

Contrary to the prediction, computers don't replace paper in the office; they just make it quicker and easier to produce more of it.

People like to handle paper. When I'm writing, for instance, I appreciate the computer editing facilities. I change things around all the time. I rephrase sentences, move whole paragraphs, insert new sections and delete others. I stand in awe of anyone who wrote before the 1980's, when personal computers started to become widely available.

But when I think I've got a chapter about right, I'll print it out. Only then do I get a feel for the whole, as I see it, feel it and read it. I'll scribble changes, reposition sentences and paragraphs, and then I'll go back to the computer, apply the changes, print it all out again, and repeat the editing cycle.

Working on a large document through the computer screen is like looking at an elephant though binoculars from a metre away. It's great for studying the detail but I can't appreciate the whole. So much for the paperless office.

The leisure society

The leisure society is an even bigger and more hideous flop than the paperless office...

The vision of the leisure society was that by the year 2000, new technology would free everyone to work fewer hours a week and get paid more money to participate in lots of new leisure activities.

Economic rationalism

Instead, economic rationalism (which is neither economic nor rational, just a euphemism used by Scrooge types for short-sighted self-interest) has meant *fewer* people now work *longer* hours for the *same* money while those whose jobs have been displaced by the new technology have *less* money.

Australians spend more time at work - and do it for free

Between 1982 and 2000, rises in average weekly working hours in Australia could have seen the creation of more than 550,000 extra full-time jobs had the work been shared with new employees. There was a 76 per cent jump in the number of people working more than 45 hours a week and a 94 per cent jump in those working 50-59 hours. One in four full-time employees, or 1.3 million workers in Australia, perform an average of 2.7 hours a week unpaid overtime. These findings are recorded in a study by RMIT University's Centre for Applied Social Research, called "Cross National Comparisons: Work Time Around the World." More than 1.6 million Australians work more than 50 hours a week - a working span unlawful in Europe. Speaking to the Industrial Relations Commission in November 2001, the ACTU advocate said that overwork was costing Australia $3 billion in fatigue-related workplace incidents and that *"most serious is the dislocation caused between parents and their children."*

The Sydney Morning Herald, November 20, 2001 (emphasis added)

People *with* jobs have *less* leisure time now, due to the pressure to keep their jobs. The little leisure time they have is disturbed more and more by the new technology that was supposed to free them up - mobile phones, pagers, faxes, e-mail, laptop computers, and so on.

People *without* jobs have the *time* but not the money to enjoy it. Somebody in the leisure society think tank forgot to consider that nobody wants to pay you to do nothing.

The Emperor has no clothes

In any case, my point is, the leisure society was flawed from the beginning. People need motivation. People need goals. People need a purpose in life, or they'll wilt and die. Mere relaxation or pleasure fulfillment can only satisfy for a short time. Suicide is prevalent among the rich and famous just as it is among the down and out.

Living in a state of constant *rest* or constant *fun* isn't a long-term proposition. And living in a state of constant *achievement* without any *rest* or *fun* will burn anybody out. All these states are good for us for short periods, but for long-term health and happiness we need to move between all three regularly.

Too much stress will kill you
And so will too little

Great stage actors still get nervous before a performance. If they get too nervous, and move from a state of healthy stress to a state of anxiety, they'll become hesitant and afraid and their performance will suffer. If they're too relaxed, they'll become complacent and they won't perform well either.

Each of us has a different capacity to deal with stress. You need to find the right balance for yourself.

The harder you push yourself, the further you'll swing from one side to the other on the pendulum and back, between extreme achievement and extreme fun. Even geniuses enjoy a bit of nonsense occasionally. Einstein must have been a fun guy.

Physical exercise, too, involves a continual cycle of pressure and release. You stretch your muscles for a short time, and then you release them for a time. Then you stretch again and release again. You keep repeating this cycle. If you over-exercise, your muscles will tear or wear out and become useless. If you under-exercise, your muscles will wither and become useless, too.

The same applies in other areas of your life. You need to keep moving, through continual pressure and release, between fun, rest and achievement, in all areas of your life - family, friends, health and hobbies - to lead a well-balanced and happy life.

Kicking an own goal

Now, a warning. Sometimes we can know it all but we're human and we still make mistakes. The worst mistake a soccer player can make is kicking an own goal. While all your team's focus, and yours, is on kicking goals at the other end of the field, a momentary slip up can result in you sending the ball into the back of your own net. It's something you and the team aren't expecting and aren't prepared for. All your team's best efforts to score at the right end can be wiped out by one mistake. It happens to the best. You even see it happen in World Cup soccer matches.

Except for the professionals, soccer is just a game. An own goal on the soccer field is embarrassing and frustrating but it can be forgiven and forgotten. But your life is not a game. If you kick an own goal in your life, you, your family or your business may have to live with the consequences forever.

In the next three chapters, I'll show you three sure-fire ways to kick an own goal and throw your life out of balance despite all your good efforts. More importantly, I'll show you how to avoid them and how to overcome them if they occur.

In the movie, *The Horse Whisperer*, based on the book by the same name, a young girl suffers a traumatic accident while horse riding. Both the girl and her horse are deeply scarred physically and emotionally. The girl's mother takes her daughter and her horse from their home in New York on the long trek to a famous horse trainer in Montana to get the girl and the horse back on track. The mother loses her job and gives everything she can to help her daughter. Then, the mother falls in love with the horse trainer and is going to leave her husband for him. Just when the daughter is turning a corner emotionally, the mother looks set to train-wreck her marriage and sabotage the emotional repair that her daughter is undergoing. That's what I call doing the hard yards and then kicking an own goal. Thankfully, at the crucial moment, the mother walks away from her temptation.

I'm a movie buff. I love movies that entertain and leave a good message - something uplifting to go on with. *The Horse Whisperer* has a happy ending but it's unsatisfying because it doesn't resolve the issues. *Cheaper by the Dozen* has a good moral and a happy ending. Towards the end, in the hilarious 2003 remake of the 1950 classic, Steve Martin's character Tom Baker and his wife Kate, played by Bonnie Hunt, are both finally living their dream careers… but at the cost of their family's happiness. Father Tom sees that his family is going to hell, so he decides to quit the high-rolling lifestyle, cash his chips in and take a necessary step back from the precipice of marriage meltdown. In quitting his dream job, he says to his boss (and I paraphrase) "I'm living my dream in this job, but if I lose my family, nothing I achieve here will matter to me anymore."

One of the best movies I've seen for couples having a hard time in their marriage is *The Story of Us,* starring Bruce Willis and Michelle Pfeiffer. It's an intense, adults-only watch. It's realistic, frustrating, extremely coarse and at times humorous, but this *sow's ear* of a movie has two *silk purse* moments. The first I've already mentioned in chapter one is the "Hi-Lo" around the family dinner table. The second is the ending, when Michelle Pfeiffer's character, Katie, makes this last ditch, rambling, emotional, tear jerking plea to save the marriage…

> "We're an *us*. There's a history here and histories don't happen overnight. You know, in Mesopotamia or somewhere back there, there are cities built on top of other cities but I don't want to build another city. I like this city. I know where we keep the… (and) what kind of mood you're in when you wake up, by which eyebrow is higher. And you always know that I'm a little quiet in the morning and compensate accordingly. That's a dance you perfect over time. And it's hard, it's much harder than I thought it would be but there's more good than bad and you don't just *give up*. And it's not for the sake of the children but they're, O God they're great kids aren't they, I mean, God, and we made them, I mean think about that, it's like there were no people there and then there were people and then they grew and I won't be able to say to some stranger, "Josh has your

hair," and "remember how Erin threw up at the Lincoln Memorial?" Then I'll try to relate. Let's face it, anybody's going to have traits that get on your nerves, I mean why shouldn't it be *your* annoying traits. And I know how to get to the beach but I do have a good sense of direction so at least I can find the beach, which is *not* a criticism of yours, it's just a strength of mine and God you're a good friend and good friends are hard to find... I love the way you read to Erin and you take on the voice of Wilbur the Pig with such commitment even when you're both tired. That speaks volumes about character and ultimately isn't that what it comes down to, what a person's made of, because that girl in the pith helmet is still in here, pee-boo, pee-boo. I didn't even know she existed until I met you and I'm afraid if you leave I may never see her again, even though I said at times you beat her out of me. Isn't that the paradox, haven't we hit the essential paradox, give and take, push and pull, yin and yang, the best of times, the worst of times, I think Dickens said it, the Jack Sprat of it, he said he could eat no fat, his wife could eat no lean, but it doesn't really apply here. I guess what I'm trying to say is... I love you."

"I love you too."

"...I'm thinking seven words: and they lived mostly happily ever after."

"I hope so."

"I think so."

"Think so?"

"I do."

"I do, too."

(Transcribed from the soundtrack of *The Story of Us*, 1999 CR Films)

You need to keep moving, through continual pressure and release, between fun, rest and achievement, in all areas of your life - family, friends, health and hobbies - to lead a well-balanced and happy life.

Chapter 6 - Down in the dumps

Getting *down in the dumps* is a sure-fire way to kick an own goal and throw your life out of balance.

It's like jumping off at the bottom of the pendulum's swing, which is the point of rest, and getting stuck in the mud. You can't get back to balance because you've fallen off the ride.

Another word for being down in the dumps is *depression*. There's no sense of fun there. There's no sense of achievement. Worst of all, there's no sense of *hope*. You can't see how you can possibly get up out of the mud and back onto the ride. You feel *hopeless*.

Hope

A hope of something better, and a plan to fulfill that hope, are essential to lift your spirit and pull you up out of the mud.

There was a time years ago when I was well and truly down in the dumps. I was worn down, worn out and depressed about every aspect of my life. What I needed was a holiday. I hadn't had a good holiday for about two years, since starting my own business. The problem was that I couldn't afford the time or the money to take one, but considering the impact my condition was having on the priority areas of my life - my family, friends, health and other interests, all of which I was neglecting in my depressed state - I came to the conclusion that I had more to lose if I *didn't* take a holiday.

So, I booked myself in for a four-week holiday to get away from work and everything else that was crowding in on me. But I didn't just go to sit on the beach. I'd started writing this book and got too busy to finish it. I decided to take the opportunity to finish the book on my holiday. To me that would be more refreshing than doing nothing. The way I'm wired, I can't think of *nothing*. I need some directed activity in order to relax.

Within 24 hours of making the call to book my holiday, two wonderful and unexpected things happened. First, money came from an unexpected source that was exactly the amount I needed to pay for my holiday. Praise God! Second, although my holiday didn't start for another month, I immediately began to feel better about the things that were getting me down. The hope of something good to come and having a plan to achieve it were enough to lift my spirit, pull me up out of the mud, and back onto the ride. When the holiday actually started, I almost felt I didn't need to go. But I did and I returned fully recharged.

Call it a *vision*, a *mission*, a *dream*, a *hope*, a *plan*, or a *goal*. Sometimes we use these words interchangeably, although each has a different meaning. In this chapter, I use the word *hope*, because when we think of depression and of being down in the dumps, the word *hopeless* comes first to mind. Now, when I write of having hope, I don't mean mere wishful thinking. You can wish all you like and nothing will happen. We don't live in Disneyland. Try singing this to yourself…

When you wish upon a star,
you will stay just where you are!

I don't mean that kind of hope. I mean the kind of hope that comes from the Hebrew word *towcheleth,* which is translated as *hope* but means *expectation.* It's pronounced "toe" (like the only part of your foot you *don't* use to kick a soccer ball) + "que" (like Manuel in Fawlty Towers says when he doesn't understand) + "leth" (like a lisper says when you ask if he wants more marzipan in his chocolate assortment). It was Solomon who wrote, in the Book of Proverbs,

Hope deferred makes the heart sick,
but when the desire comes, it is a tree of life [11]
and
Where there is no vision, the people perish [12]

---

[11] Proverbs 13:12 "*Hope deferred makes the heart sick, but when the desire comes, it is a tree of life.*"
[12] Proverbs 29:18 "*Where there is no vision, the people perish*" (King James Version)

Hope without a plan to fulfill that hope is not *towcheleth* hope. Hope without a plan is just wishful thinking. It won't overcome depression because you can't fool yourself with it. In chapter two, I introduced the acronym SMART to describe good goals. SMART stands for Specific, Measurable, Achievable, Results-oriented and Time-driven. *Towcheleth* is SMART hope. A SMART plan turns wishful thinking into expectation, or *towcheleth.* Without a SMART plan, you have no expectation of achieving the thing you hope for.

If you fail to plan,
you plan to fail

In the week before I went away on holiday, I prepared a Business Plan for a small business owner client of mine. Before she had the plan, she had no idea how her business was going or where it was headed. A quick financial analysis revealed the business was going backwards and headed for closure within weeks unless a plan was formulated to rescue it and turn it around. The owner *wished* the business would succeed, but without a plan nothing of the sort was going to happen. The planning process identified reasons for the losses and the means of turning the business to profit. Now the owner has a hope and a plan to fulfill that hope. Now she has *towcheleth!* Now she knows what she needs to do to succeed. And it's achievable.

Based solely on that Business Plan, her bank granted an overdraft to keep the business afloat while the owner works the plan. If she went to the bank with her problem and no plan, there's no way the bank would lend money because they would have no *towcheleth* of getting their money back. The bank understands *towcheleth* and is willing to bet its own money on it!

Before the owner had a plan, she had no hope. Now that she has a plan, she has confidence in her business, hope for the future, and the bank's money to help her get there!

Do you want to know what I put into that plan, that so impressed the bank? I didn't start with the financial analysis. In fact, the financial analysis started on page 19. At the front of the plan, I wrote a Vision statement, Mission statement, Values and Goals for the business. Then, I wrote a SWOT analysis of the business and a SWOT analysis for each of the key individuals, in this case the owner and each staff member. Because they are a wonderful help to get an individual or a business out of the dumps, I'll explain each of these terms a little more in the following pages.

Before I do, why do you suppose I put those things first in the Business Plan? The reason is that they represent the *priorities* of the business. We talked about the importance of priorities in chapter one. If you want to succeed in business, as in personal life, you have to put *first things first.* Every other action or decision has to come after them, be guided by them, and its effectiveness measured by them.

The **Vision** statement

The Vision statement is your ultimate ideal. It's like a long-term goal but it's more than a goal. A good Vision statement is something that can *ever* be approached but *never* fully attained.

Use the worksheet (Worksheet 4) below to write your personal Vision statement. If you have a business, use a separate page to write a Vision statement for your business.

Figure 8 - **Worksheet 4: My Vision**

The **Mission** statement

The Mission statement describes your core activity, what you do, your purpose in life, your raison d'être. It should be long enough to be meaningful but short enough to be memorable. Use the next worksheet (Worksheet 5) to write your personal Mission statement.

If you have a business, use a separate page to write a Mission statement for your business. The Mission statement is for the people in and around the business. It is they who must feel the energy it describes, the very purpose for which the business exists.

Figure 9 - **Worksheet 5: My Mission**

The **Values** statement

Plans and goals will develop and change over time. Occasionally, you might even need to revise your vision and your mission statements. However, Values are those things that are non-negotiable, inviolable. They cannot be compromised or sacrificed for the attainment of either short-term or long-term goals. Their over-riding importance is held to be self-evident. Values are the constants around which all your other plans and activities centre.

Use the worksheet (Worksheet 6) below to write your personal Values statement. If you have a business, use a separate page to write a Values statement for your business.

Figure 10 - **Worksheet 6: My Values**

Goals

Goals are specific objectives that are consistent with your Vision, Mission and Values. Good goals are SMART goals. SMART stands for Specific, Measurable, Achievable, Results-oriented and Time-driven.

You may have already written down your personal goals in chapter two. If not, or if you want to do them again to improve or compare, you can use the next worksheet (Worksheet 7). If you have a business, use a separate page to write your Goals for your business.

Include both short-term and long-term goals. If possible, include a goal you can achieve this week, another you can achieve in one to three months and another in twelve months. Go longer if you can.

Figure 11 - **Worksheet 7: My Goals**

SWOT analysis

SWOT is an acronym that stands for Strengths, Weaknesses, Opportunities and Threats. You can do a SWOT analysis for yourself and another for your business if you have one. First, make a list of your Strengths and then a list of your Weaknesses. These are internal attributes and shouldn't be hard to identify, provided you're honest with yourself. When thinking about Opportunities to write down, think of external things that you can capitalise on, and creative ways of capitalising on your strengths. When thinking about Threats to write down, think of external things that may hurt you, or ways in which your weaknesses could hurt you. Finally, think about creative ways to avoid or overcome your weaknesses and threats, then write these down.

The SWOT analysis was the trigger for most of the helpful suggestions that went into the Business Plan that my client's bank so liked. We touch again on Strengths and Weaknesses in the next two chapters. In the meantime, you can use the following worksheets (Worksheets 8, 9, 10 and 11) to do a personal SWOT analysis. If you have a business, do a separate SWOT analysis for it.

Figure 12 - **Worksheet 8: My Strengths**

What they are	How I can capitalise on them

Figure 13 - **Worksheet 9: My Weaknesses**

What they are	How I can avoid or overcome them

Figure 14 - **Worksheet 10: My Opportunities**

What they are	How I can capitalise on them

Figure 15 - **Worksheet 11: My Threats**

What they are	How I can avoid or overcome them

Common Cents

A common cause of depression, which I'll deal with next, is unemployment or under-employment. I've been in this position. I became "Mr Mom" for three years while my children were in primary school and my wife worked full-time, *à la* the movie *Mr Mom* starring Michael Keaton. That turned out to be an important and rewarding stage of our family's growth. A number of lessons shared in earlier chapters I learned during those years.

Prevention is always better than cure. Unemployment isn't always preventable, but if you've got a job you want to keep, here are five, simple, common sense hints that may help you prevent unemployment.

DUMPS PREVENTION NUMBER ONE

Don't burn yourself out

Knock off work on time. I don't mean you should become a clock-watcher. Remember you're paid for your work, not your attendance. I mean don't get into a habit of working late. It might impress your boss for a while but it will soon become expected and then you can't ever go back. If you've gotten into a habit of working until six, then you start knocking off at five, you'll be perceived as becoming slack. Unfair but true.

Bosses, don't burn your staff out and don't let them do it to themselves. It's false economy. The cost of losing a good employee is staggering in terms of business downtime, service disruption, rehiring costs, retraining costs and lost custom depending on the nature of the employee's duties and responsibilities.

There's no point working so hard that you burn yourself out. When you do, your employer will have to get rid of you and you'll be no good to anybody else. Better to work within your capacity, and if that's not good enough for your employer then look for another job.

If you're your own boss, the same still applies. Don't burn yourself out. Give 100% but know when to quit. At the end of the day, tune out to work and tune in to your other interests - your family, friends, health and hobbies.

DUMPS PREVENTION NUMBER TWO

Don't milk your privileges

If you start at nine o'clock in the morning, arrive at quarter to nine. Most people spend at least the first fifteen minutes after arriving socialising and getting ready to work, but not actually doing anything productive. You're paid for your work, not your attendance.

Don't milk your privileges. Don't abuse your liberties. *Don't shake the money tree, lest the leaves fall off and it stops bearing fruit.* Don't be one of those employees who are always whingeing or forever trying to get something for nothing. Don't steal time from your employer. Don't view your relationship as between "us" and "them." We're all "us." Our interests coincide. The business needs to make a profit to keep employing you. If you abuse that relationship, you may be kicking an own goal, because you may ultimately suffer for it. Maybe your employer acts like he doesn't understand this himself. If so, he's the dummy. Don't follow his lead.

DUMPS PREVENTION NUMBER THREE

Under-commit and over-deliver

Don't be a "Yes" man. If you can't do an assignment, or if a deadline is unachievable, say so. To say "Yes" or to say nothing is to commit employment suicide. If you speak up at the beginning, other options can be explored. But if the deadline arrives and the job isn't done, your boss is out of options and will be most upset with you. If you're your own boss, the same applies, only worse: you'll have no one else to blame and you alone will suffer the consequences.

When I was a project manager with IBM, I was fond of telling my staff that a project can only get late a day at a time. In other words, they should tell me of a problem as soon as they suspect it, so the damage can be minimised before it snowballs into a bigger problem.

If you think you can finish a job by Thursday, promise it by Friday to allow for contingencies and deliver it Thursday if you can, or Friday at the latest. Give your employer or your client a *pleasant* surprise. Apply the same principle to your costings. Imagine the smile on your boss's or client's face when the actual cost is *less* than quoted!

DUMPS PREVENTION NUMBER FOUR

Be enthusiastic

Don't be a "No" Man. Be enthusiastic about your job. Accept reasonable instructions and assignments willingly and cheerfully. Make your employer's life easier. Be a pleasure to have around.

DUMPS PREVENTION NUMBER FIVE

Make yourself more valuable

Learn a new skill or do some research related to your industry at least once a year. You'll get more job satisfaction and you'll insure yourself against redundancy.

So much for prevention. As for the cure, if you're unemployed or under-employed, here are seven hints that should help you use your time to advantage and get you back on your feet.

DUMPS CURE NUMBER ONE

Budget your time

Set a target for the number of hours you'll spend in a week looking for employment. Spend those hours reading job ads and going to employment agents and job interviews. Don't spend your entire time job-hunting for any extended period, because repeated failure can make you even more depressed. Stick to the budgeted hours and use the rest of your time to do other things, like…

DUMPS CURE NUMBER TWO

Make yourself more valuable

Learn a new skill or do some research related to your industry. You'll be even more valuable to your next employer than you were to your last one.

DUMPS CURE NUMBER THREE

Spend more time on your other interests and hobbies

If you don't have a consuming interest aside from your job or your business, get one. Like I said in chapter one, asking yourself these questions might help you find one: *What gets you really motivated? When you're tired, what sparks action or interest in you? What do you like to read about? What is it, once you start talking about it, you can't stop? What will get you up at three o'clock in the morning?*

DUMPS CURE NUMBER FOUR

Make up for lost time with your family

This is your big chance. Use your time as an asset. Don't waste it.

DUMPS CURE NUMBER FIVE

Tell your friends and associates what you're doing

This is an important time when you need their company and their support. They might even know someone who needs a new employee like you. Word of mouth is still the most effective form of advertising. A good referral is better than a dozen cold interviews.

DUMPS CURE NUMBER SIX

Take a well-earned break

If you haven't had a holiday in ages, take one now while you can, because your next job won't let you for another twelve months.

DUMPS CURE NUMBER SEVEN

Take up a new exercise regime

Do it while you have more time available.

In short, if you're unemployed or under-employed, treat your newfound time as an *asset* and make good use of it.

To wrap this up, I'll use another sporting analogy. A soccer player who finds himself on the bench more often than on the playing field has three choices: he can give up; he can train harder; or he can look for a transfer to another club that will make better use of his skills and knowledge. That about sums up your choices, too. If you're down in the dumps, you can give up (not a good option), you can work on improving yourself or your circumstances, or you can move on.

Finally, make a list of things that get you down. Beside each one, write what you can do to avoid it pulling you down or to pick yourself up if it does. You can use the worksheet below (Worksheet 12).

If you continue kicking own goals and getting down in the dumps, you may benefit from more professional help. That's nothing to be embarrassed about. All of us can benefit at one time or another from wise counsel in some area of our life. It's not uncommon to have problems. *It's only uncommon to do something sensible about them!* I suggest you start with your local church minister. Many of them are trained in counselling. They provide a non-threatening environment and most are happy to provide their services free of charge. If you're uncomfortable with your local minister, try another. None should be offended to be asked; in fact they should be pleased to know you're seeking help. Alternatively, ask your doctor for a referral.

Figure 16 - **Worksheet 12: Things that get me down**

What they are	How I can avoid or overcome them

1. Have a hope of something better and a plan to fulfill it

2. If you fail to plan, you plan to fail

3. Write your Vision, Mission, Values, Goals and SWOT

4. Treat your time as an *asset* and make good use of it

Five ways to prevent unemployment

Don't burn yourself out
Don't milk your privileges
Under-commit and over-deliver
Be enthusiastic
Make yourself more valuable

Seven ways to deal with unemployment

Budget your time
Make yourself more valuable
Spend more time on your other interests and hobbies

Common Cents

Make up for lost time with your family
Tell your friends and associates what you're doing
Take a well-earned break
Take up a new exercise regime

Chapter 7 - Overcoming your weaknesses

Giving in to temptation is a sure-fire way to kick an own goal and throw your life out of balance.

It's like swinging off to the far-left side of the pendulum, the *fun* or pleasure side, and letting go. You can't get back to balance because you've fallen off the ride.

A temptation is some irresistible impulse, compulsion or obsession that's not good for you.

It's not a sin to be tempted,
only to give in

If you know *not* to do something but, when tempted, you still do it, you've kicked an own goal.

For instance, if you've really got your priorities in balance and you're growing in every area of your life, but you have too many drinks one night and have an accident in your car coming home, you goofed. You kicked an own goal.

A possible consequence of this one goof could be financial ruin, because you ran into another car, totalled both it and your own car, and the insurance company won't pay because you were over the legal blood alcohol limit. Another consequence of this one goof could be lifelong emotional trauma for you and your family, knowing that you killed someone's daughter or someone's mother. You might have to pay the additional costs of moving to another suburb or town to avoid vilification. Another consequence of this one goof could be that you're dead.

What a waste of time and money. With one mistake, you could ruin everything you've been building up until now. *That's* an own goal.

If you're really working hard at teaching your kids good values and censoring sex and violence on the television in your home, but you have a one-night affair at the annual office party, you goofed. You kicked an own goal.

A consequence of this one goof could be that you can no longer work together effectively with the other person and, directly or indirectly, you lose your job. Another consequence of this one goof could be a ruined marriage and a split family. Another consequence could be that you contract a transmittable disease and die.

What a waste of time and money. With one mistake, you could ruin everything you've been building up until now. *That's* an own goal.

Ears may be closed to advice,
but eyes are always open to example

If you willingly leave your spouse and children for another partner, you're kicking an own goal. By your action, you're telling your own kids, and other kids who watch you too, that sex and self-gratification are more important than love and commitment. You're telling them that your word, your wedding vow, *"'til death us do part", isn't* your bond. You're setting a bad example for them to follow. And follow it they will.

The Law of Copy Cat

Remember, people are generally quite well balanced. On average, they'll follow a *good* example about *half* as good and they'll follow a *bad* example about *twice* as bad! I call this the *Law of Copy Cat.*

Unequally yoked

If you're judicious and scrupulous with your financial dealings but you're tempted to take on a project with a dubious partner because you think there could be a lot of money to be made, you're kicking an own goal. The apostle Paul writing his second letter to the Corinthians called this being *"unequally yoked."* [13] The yoke Paul refers to in his metaphor is a heavy wooden brace placed around the neck of a pair of oxen pulling a cart or a plough. If the oxen work in

---

[13] 2nd Corinthians 6:14 *"Do not be unequally yoked together"*

unison, they share the load equally and can achieve much. If they pull in different directions, the yoke becomes unequal. An unequal yoke is a painful burden to both animals and prevents them from achieving anything.

Don't allow yourself to be yoked or tied or dependent on someone you don't trust implicitly. As a test, before tying yourself to a partner, whether in business or in any other sense, ask yourself, "Would I feel safe giving this person access to my bank accounts and credit cards for a week?" because if the partnership ends in tears, that's what you stand to lose and more.

Judge people by their character,
not their gifting

Leopards don't change their spots. If this new partner is, as suspected, of dubious character, he'll bite you back eventually and you'll go to your financial grave saying things like "I should have trusted my instincts" and "I should have known better."

One mistake could ruin everything you've been building up until now. *That's* an own goal.

One of the most often misquoted people of all time is the Scottish philosopher Francis Hutcheson (1694-1746) who wrote,

"Wisdom denotes the pursuing
of the best ends by the best means" [14]

---

[14] *An Inquiry into the Original of our Ideas of Beauty and Virtue* (1725) Treatise I, sect. 5, subsect. 16; found in: The Oxford Dictionary of Quotations, fifth edition, #396:14.

The popular misquoting, which completely reverses the meaning, is "the ends justify the means."

Later, the French novelist and political writer Georges Bernanos (1888-1948) wrote,

"The first sign of corruption in a society that is still alive is that the end justifies the means" [15]

Ends do *not* justify means. Don't be tempted to lie or cheat in order to achieve something good. For example, you wouldn't rob a bank to donate money to charity. The example isn't as silly or remote as it sounds. We all face similar but more subtle temptations every day. For instance, some people cheat or avoid tax so they can give the money to charity. Now, the government treasury isn't going to miss out, so that means *you* have to pay more tax to compensate for those people's charity. They're robbing *your* bank to donate money to *their* charity. But they're not Robin Hood, and you're not the Sheriff of Nottingham!

Judas Iscariot was an enemy of the Roman State in the early first century. Contrary to his principles, in a moment of foolishness, he put himself in league with the Roman authorities and accepted blood money to betray his faithful friend Jesus. He wrongly thought advantage would be gained for his cause. Too late, he realised he had been deluded. He'd kicked an own goal. He threw the money away in a field and hung himself from a tree. What a waste of time and money.

---

[15] www.bartleby.com/66/61/6961

Here's a helpful suggestion. If in doubt as to the ethics of a particular decision or action, ask yourself:

Would I be happy to explain my actions to anyone who asks?

If not, don't do it. Don't risk compromising your integrity or your reputation.

A good reputation is slow to achieve and quick to lose

If you want to be a positive influence within your family, your workplace, your business, or your community, you need to be beyond reproach.

Lead by example

Be someone that people can look up to and trust. For example, if you run a business and you put some sales through without ringing them up on the till or issuing an invoice, you're encouraging your staff to cheat too. You are their leader. Ask yourself, "Where am I leading them?" You might trust them implicitly. They may be perfectly honest. But one day they might be processing an under-the-counter cash transaction and put the money in their pocket, mixed with their own cash, and forget part of it belongs to you. Then they'll see how easy it is and they might be tempted to do it again. Your cash is out of control. You lose. You want to *take control* of your finances, not lose it.

Worse still, don't invite them to lie, cheat or steal for you. In a well-known example, an employer told a new junior staff member to answer the phone and say he (the employer) wasn't in the office. "You tell them yourself" the employee responded, handing the receiver to his new boss. Livid, the employer later roasted the new boy. The young fellow's response has become a classic:

"If I can lie for you, I can lie to you. I will do neither."

From that moment on, that fellow became his boss's most trusted employee.

Do the right thing, first time, every time

Nowhere is this point made more clearly than in the story of *The Lord of the Rings*. It's a story of death and destruction on a massive scale caused by the existence of the evil Lord *Sauron's* One Ring and the attempts of good folk to find and destroy it. Students of the text and the movie will know that the whole exercise could have been avoided thousands of years earlier when *Aragorn's* ancestor *Isildur* had possession of the One Ring and stood poised to destroy it, which he knew was the right thing to do. However *Isildur* gave into temptation at the last instant and decided to keep the Ring for himself. Subsequently he lost it and the reign of evil in Middle Earth went on unabated for thousands of years, until *Frodo* returned to complete the job *Isildur* had failed to finish. Another aspect to this is the mercy that *Frodo* showed *Gollum*. Against all advice and apparent common sense, *Frodo* refused to do away with *Gollum*, who wanted to kill *Frodo* and keep the ring. In the end, when *Frodo* stood where *Isildur* had stood before him, poised to throw the Ring into the lake of fire, *Frodo* began to give in to the same temptation that had consumed *Isildur*, but it was *Gollum's* intervention at the last instant that indirectly destroyed the Ring and saved all of Middle Earth from total annihilation. *Isildur* was like the first Adam, who in a single weak moment stuffed up the world for thousands of years to come. *Frodo* was like the second Adam, Jesus, who satisfied both justice and mercy in finishing the job the first had begun.

Never compromise your values. Once you start to deceive, the deceptions snowball. It's the thin end of the wedge, as Sir Humphrey Appleby is fond of saying in the television series *Yes, Minister*. If you stand for nothing, you'll fall for anything.

Know what you stand for
and fall for nothing less

Write down a list of your values in life. Your values are things you believe in, things you stand for, things you aspire to be known for. Things like honesty, integrity, reliability and *your word is your bond.* You may have already written down your values in chapter six. If not, or if you want to do them again to improve or compare, you can use the next worksheet (Worksheet 13).

Your values are non-negotiable. Whatever you do, you will not violate these. Choose them carefully. Then stick to them, come what may.

Figure 17 - **Worksheet 13: My Values**

So how do you avoid kicking an own goal?

Prevention is better than cure.

Be honest with yourself about your weaknesses. For instance, are you a compulsive liar or exaggerator?

I used to exaggerate all *the time but now I* never *do*

Seriously, what temptations do you find hard to resist? Write them down.

You may have already included them when you listed your weaknesses in chapter six. If not, or if you want to do them again to improve or compare, you can use the worksheet provided (Worksheet 14). Next to each one, write down what you're going to do to avoid it or overcome it.

Give temptation a wide berth

Take exceptional measures to avoid tempting circumstances. It's not enough to be aware of them. By definition, these are things you struggle with and frequently give in to. You have to take exceptional measures to avoid them.

Don't be like the reformed drunk, who walked past the pub and prayed vainly, as he walked through its doors, "Lord, protect me from temptation." If this chap had my worksheet, then, in the first column, the list of things he found hard to resist, he'd write "Pubs." In the second column, under "How I can avoid them", he'd write: "Don't walk past a pub; when I see one, I'll cross the street or take a longer route around the block if I have to."

Figure 18 - **Worksheet 14: Temptations I find hard to resist**

What they are	How I can avoid or overcome them

If you're married and you have an attraction to someone in your workplace other than your spouse, then give temptation a wide berth: avoid meeting together, avoid working on projects together, request a transfer to another project or department, or get another job.

Drastic circumstances require drastic action. If you don't take action to avoid a temptation, it's almost inevitable you'll eventually succumb to it. The action, in this case quitting your job, may be drastic, but the consequences of doing nothing will be diabolical. And you may lose your job anyway, through additional workplace stress caused by the new relationship, or through emotional breakdown and inability to function at work due to the rift within your family. What a waste of time and money.

Picking the ball out of the back of the net

What if it's too late? What if you've kicked an own goal already?

Don't worry. It happens to the best. The apostle Paul must have kicked a few own goals in his time, based on this confession in his letter to the Roman church:

> *"For the good that I will to do, I do not do;*
> *but the evil I will not to do, that I practice."* [16]

I know how he feels. It's basic, flawed, human nature.

As in the soccer analogy, an own goal isn't always your own fault, either. The ball can be deflected off you into your own

---

[16] Romans 7:19 *"For the good that I will to do, I do not do; but the evil I will not to do, that I practice."*

goal and you can't do a thing about it. But whether it's your fault or not, the answer is the same. Figuratively speaking, you've got to pick the ball out of the back of the net and restart the game. You're behind on the scoreboard but that's not the end of the game. The winner is the one who's ahead at the end of the match, not the one who scores the first goal. Conceding a goal makes it tougher, you have to try harder, and it's tempting to get depressed and give up.

Prevention is better than cure, but when prevention fails, bring on the cure…

TEMPTATION'S CURE NUMBER ONE

Never give up

My favourite soccer match of all time is the 1999 European Cup final between Manchester United and Bayern Munich. Bayern scored a goal early in the first half, in about the seventh minute, and still led one-nil leading into stoppage time at the end of the second half. Could United salvage a last gasp goal and draw the game into extra time or a penalty shoot-out? The time indicator board went up to announce that three minutes of stoppage time would be played to compensate for time lost attending to injuries and other interruptions during the regulation ninety minutes of the match.

One minute into stoppage time, United scored an exciting, surprise goal. The impossible had happened and the teams were level. But, as you know, miracles take a little longer, and one and a half minutes later, United scored a second goal. They won the match, the cup, and the unbelievable treble of winning the English Premier League, the FA Cup and the European Cup in the one year. Unbelievably, United went *from zero to hero* within one and a half minutes, scoring two goals after being scoreless for the first ninety-one minutes.

How sweet that victory was! It's a wonderful illustration to prove the point that even though you're down you're never out until you give up trying.

Manchester United were the losers for eighty-four minutes out of the ninety-three minutes in that match. They had to live with the consequences of that early goal against them. But they didn't give up, and then, in a final rush of adrenalin, they not only caught up with the past but also came out winners. That victory was the sweetest of all.

I never wish tragedy to befall you, but it's true in life that often the greatest victories rise from the ashes of defeat.

TEMPTATION'S CURE NUMBER TWO

Stop what you're doing wrong

Don't make it worse. Don't do it again.

Don't be like the chocoholic who eats a spoonful of chocolate ice cream, then suffers a severe attack of guilt and depression and so eats the rest of the tub in response to the depression. That's tempting but self-defeating.

Employ the aforementioned preventative measures doubly so, to avoid repeating the folly. Use the worksheet prepared several pages back (Worksheet 14) to prepare a stronger plan to avoid temptation in future.

TEMPTATION'S CURE NUMBER THREE

Get help from your family and friends

Form an accountability group with a couple of close friends.

Choose people you trust to put your interests first. Choose people you trust to give you sound advice. Choose people you trust to keep your confidence and not gossip.

Meet with them regularly to discuss how you've been dealing with your temptation since your last meeting.

Groups like Alcoholics Anonymous and Gamblers Anonymous follow this basic pattern. If you can't get the help you need from family and friends, seek out professional help from a counsellor or a self-help group such as these.

TEMPTATION'S CURE NUMBER FOUR

Seek forgiveness

Guilt and shame are a debilitating burden, a yoke around your neck. Forgiveness alone has the power to set you free.

If possible, without offending or hurting them any more, approach people you've offended or hurt and ask their forgiveness. Don't be concerned by their response. When you do this, you're operating in grace, but they might not be ready to respond in kind. *They* might not be ready to forgive *you*. That's not your problem. You've released the yoke from your neck. Their time might come later.

There is a catch, however. If you want something, you have to give it away (see chapter nine). If you want to be forgiven, you have to learn to forgive others first. Recite the Lord's Prayer to yourself. You'll find it in chapter six of the book of Matthew in any Bible. The key phrase is, *"forgive us our debts, as we forgive our debtors,"* [17] or in some versions, *"forgive us our trespasses, as we forgive those who trespass against us."* Ouch! That means you can't be a hypocrite. A hypocrite wants to be forgiven his faults but won't forgive others. If you want to find forgiveness, you have to learn to forgive others first.

Worry is often associated with guilt and shame. I guess that's why Matthew deals with them together. Worry is an awful waste of time and money. *"Which of you by worrying can add one cubit to his stature?"* [18] Matthew rightly asks. Worry

---

[17] Matthew 6:12 *"forgive us our debts, as we forgive our debtors."*
[18] Matthew 6:27 *"Which of you by worrying can add one cubit to his stature?"*

consumes its victims and helps them achieve nothing. It's a common problem and a perfectly senseless waste of time and money. It's common senseless!

I find the practice of carrying a pen and paper in my pocket everywhere I go helps me get things off my mind and stop worrying about them. I mentioned this at the beginning of chapter two. Sometimes writing down the worst thing that can happen and then the best thing that can happen helps me get things in better perspective. If I'm worrying about a decision I have to make, or a problem I have to solve, the pen and paper in my pocket lets me draw a mind map there and then (see chapter ten).

Repeated studies and surveys show that people worry more about public speaking than about anything else including death. Perhaps that's because if you muck up a speaking engagement, first you die of embarrassment, then you die every time you relive it. At least with physical death you only die once! Public speaking is an important skill in community and business life, so I've written a few hints that might help you…

It should comfort you to know that, above all, what you have to do is relax and *be yourself.* People enjoy hearing *you* more than what you have to say. Use abbreviated notes. If you have full text notes, you'll be tempted to read them word for word. Audiences hate that and tune out. They can read the notes themselves. They want to hear *you!* If you try to be someone else, they'll lose interest in you and won't hear what you say. If you just relax and be yourself, they'll relax and listen more to what you say. Better to be yourself and muck up or forget a few lines while keeping the audience's attention than read your notes perfectly and have them fall asleep half way through.

Think of great speakers and speeches you've heard – people like British Prime Minister Winston Churchill, speaking to the House of Commons in 1940 after the retreat from Dunkirk during World War II:

> *"We shall fight on the beaches, we shall fight on the landing grounds, we shall fight in the fields and in the streets, we shall fight in the hills; we shall never surrender."* [19]

… and American President John F Kennedy, in his 1961 inauguration address:

> *"My fellow Americans, ask not what your country can do for you—ask what you can do for your country… My fellow citizens of the world, ask not what America will do for you, but what together we can do for the freedom of man."* [20]

… and American civil rights leader Martin Luther King Jr, in his 1963 public address at the Lincoln Memorial:

> *"I have a dream that my four little children will one day live in a nation where they will not be judged by the colour of their skin, but by the content of their character."* [21]

---

[19] www.bartleby.com/66/59/12359
[20] www.bartleby.com/66/31/32431
[21] www.bartleby.com/63/19/5119

The *way* they say it is as memorable as *what* they say. It's like telling a joke - often the way it's told is what makes it so funny and so memorable. I can remember the lyrics of a song, or the rhyming words of a poem, but I can't remember a five-item shopping list! You don't have to speak like Winston Churchill to get your point across, nor do you have to drone on like a mindless automaton. Just be yourself!

Definition of a fanatic

I have a bad habit of pausing and experiencing a sudden surge of self-doubt after talking for about twenty minutes. Then I remember the definition of a fanatic. A fanatic is someone who, as soon as he loses sight of his objective, doubles his effort. That's what I do when I pause and panic. I decide I'm fanatical about my message and I double my effort. It works for me.

TEMPTATION'S CURE NUMBER FIVE

Restore what's been lost to those you've hurt

This may not always be possible. In some cases, it may not even be advisable. But, if possible, make an appropriate effort. Even a token effort, if that's all that is possible, is significant. Perform an anonymous act of charity that they would never suspect you of. Whatever form it takes, the important thing is that it's an admission of your sorrow, and it's a sign, to yourself and perhaps others too, that you've changed. You've turned a corner.

Yeah But…

Finally, there is one temptation you should always give in to… the temptation to do something good!

Most of us need a good kick in our *Yeah But.* That's the part of us that stops us doing good deeds. We're quick to justify doing something that's bad for us or bad for others and we're equally quick to justify *not* doing something that's good. We say to ourselves, "*Yeah But…* he'll probably think I'm a goody-goody or a show-off"… "*Yeah But…* she might not like that colour"… "*Yeah But…* it might inconvenience me" and so on. Give yourself a good kick in your *Yeah But.* Give in quickly to the temptation to do something good!

1. Identify your weaknesses and make plans to avoid or overcome them
2. Give temptation a wide berth
3. Don't allow yourself to become unequally yoked
4. Judge people by their character, not their gifting
5. Wisdom denotes the pursuing of the best ends by the best means
6. Would I be happy to explain my actions to anyone?
7. Do the right thing, first time, every time
8. Know what you stand for and fall for nothing less
9. Never give up
10. Stop what you're doing wrong
11. Get help from your family and friends
12. Seek forgiveness
13. Restore what's been lost to those you've hurt
14. Give yourself a good kick in your *Yeah But* and give in to the temptation to do something good

Chapter 8 - Building on your strengths

Your success will come from your strengths, so build on your strengths. Don't waste what you've got through complacency or neglect, or what I call having your head in the clouds. Having your head in the clouds is a sure-fire way to kick an own goal and throw your life out of balance.

It's like swinging off to the far-right side, the *achievement* side, of the pendulum introduced in chapter five, and letting go. You can't get back to balance because you've fallen off the ride.

She'll be right

Having your head in the clouds is delusion. It's over-confidence. It's complacency. It's pride. It's arrogance. It's an attitude of "She'll be right, mate." It's an attitude of "I can do anything."

If you *know* to do something but you *don't* do it, and then you suffer as a result, that's an own goal. You've got your head in the clouds. You goofed.

When you say, *"I should have known better,"* what you mean is that you *did* know better but were complacent and didn't follow up on your own common sense.

You can be complacent or have your head in the clouds about weaknesses too. For instance, if you know your weakest link is your marriage, but don't work on it, and you end up in divorce, you goofed. You kicked an own goal.

If you know you need exercise, but you do nothing about it and end up having a heart attack, you goofed. You kicked an own goal.

If you think your kids can make up their own minds about their life choices and about right and wrong, you're deluded. If they could, the advertising industry wouldn't exist.

If you think your kids are better off with one parent than two who fight, you're wrong - they're better off with two parents who can work out their differences. Gee, you made it this far, don't give up now! By giving up too easily on your marriage, you're telling your kids that it's ok to give up in any aspect of life when the going gets tough or you feel like a change. By giving up too easily on your marriage, you're telling them that you lied when you gave your wedding vows. When you married "for better or worse" you meant "while things are going well." When you married "til death us do part" you meant "til I feel otherwise." They'll follow your example. Be a good example in every aspect of your life, for their sake, and don't confuse true love with infatuation. Infatuation is self-centred. It's a *feeling* that can go as quickly as it comes. True love is self-*less*.

True love is a decision to act selflessly,
regardless of how you feel.

Like layers of plywood bonded together, you can't separate a family without tearing the components, because the bonding process fuses the parts into a brand new whole.

Your true love is not just your partner,
your true love is a ***part of you****.*

Now don't get me wrong. If it's over, it's over. That's *history* and that's *not* what I'm on about. What I'm on about is early intervention and getting your life in balance *now*.

When I was a project manager with IBM, I learnt that close monitoring of trends in just three basic areas can avert most problems. The three are: time, money and quality. How does a project become a month late? Answer: *one day at a time*. How does a project go a million dollars over budget? Answer: *one dollar at a time*. How does a product accumulate a hundred defects? Answer: *one mistake at a time*. The point is that regular monitoring of these three basic areas can avert major problems developing.

Look after little problems,
before they become big problems

Don't shoot the messenger. I reward employees who bring problems to me at their earliest stage. That's why they say:

The customer is always right

Customer feedback is cheap market research. For every customer who does you the favour of complaining, there are probably ten or ten times ten who didn't bother. Instead, they're out telling everyone else, to your detriment. The one who comes to you is like gold! You should kiss them. Even if their complaint is wrong or unjustified, it's better business to treat them as being right. Perception is everything to them. Unless they're being deliberately dishonest, they really think they're right and if you try to convince them otherwise they'll just think you're trying to fob them off. Then when they have a *real* complaint, they won't bring it to you. Good problem resolution is a marketing feather in your cap. If you handle complaints well, complainants can become your best ambassadors. So, whether they're customers, employees, friends, or family, don't make people afraid to bring you bad news.

Early warning systems

Early warning systems are imperative in every area of your life, not just business. Look out for early symptoms of problems in your family, between friends, in your health, and nip them in the bud. Don't let the sun go down on an unresolved issue. Don't assume that "she'll be right." Don't allow yourself to be deluded. There's a basic principle at work in all these examples:

If you're faithful in the little things,
the big things will look after themselves

If you're quick to spot *little* problems and fix them promptly, you'll get fewer *big* problems.
It's like weeding your garden. The little weeds seem too *small* to bother about. But if you turn your back on them, the

next time you look at your garden, it's a jungle of weeds and now the problem seems too *big* to cope with! The moral of the story is that it's easier in the long run to deal with little problems before they become big problems. Like children.

If you want to do something big with your life one day, start with something small that you can do today. If you want to give a million dollars to charity when you're rich, start by giving ten dollars when you're poor. If you won't give ten dollars now, you won't give a million later. Learn to walk before you run.

Build on your strengths. Don't waste what you've got, through complacency or neglect. Your success will come from your strengths. I sometimes see people who are gifted in one area give that up or put it aside to try something else and they fail and get depressed.

Do well what you do best

Take a leaf out of the Chinese ping-pong players' training manual. The Chinese are the best ping-pong players in the world. They dominate world championship titles and rankings. What makes the difference between the Chinese and the rest of the world is the way they train. Other players spend most of their training working on their weaknesses. For instance, an Australian with a weak backhand will train to improve his backhand. The Chinese spend most of their training improving on their strengths. A Chinese with a weak backhand will train to improve his forehand. The result is a dynamite forehand that rarely or barely gets returned, so his weaker backhand rarely gets tested!

The best ping-pong players in the world get to be the best by building on their strengths. Of course you have to consider your weaknesses and make plans to contain the threats they pose. Otherwise, your strengths could be undermined. That's just good risk management. But your success will not come merely from avoiding failure. It will come from building on your strengths.

Identify your strengths, gifts and talents. You may have already written down your strengths in chapter six. If not, or if you want to do them again to improve or compare, you can use the worksheet (Worksheet 15) at the end of this chapter. Then think of ways to capitalise or build on each strength and write these down in the second column.

Stick to the knitting

In the classic management book, *In Search of Excellence*, the authors list common traits of companies who excel. One of the common traits of all the excellent companies the authors study is that these companies "stick to the knitting." They write their vision, mission, goals and values and they stick to them without wavering. They don't say, "Let's do this or let's do that." They say, "This is what we do *best*. Let's see how we can do it *better*." They focus on doing *well* what they do *best*.

Strength to strength

Finally, don't start a new project or business venture until you've got your present ones and your finances under control. Build from strength to strength, not from weakness to weakness. Stick to the knitting, too - you can't assume that success in one field will assure you success in a different field. Successful diversification is rare.

Figure 19 - **Worksheet 15: My Strengths**

What they are	How I can build on them

1. Don't waste what you've got through complacency or neglect
2. If you're faithful in the little things, the big things will look after themselves
3. Look for early warning signs
4. Nip problems in the bud
5. Don't let the sun go down on unresolved issues
6. If you want to do something big, start by doing something small that you can do now
7. Do *well* what you do *best*
8. Stick to the knitting
9. Build on your strengths
10. Build from strength *to* strength

Chapter 9 – Being a cheerful giver

In this chapter, I'm going to show you how to think outside the box. Look at Diagram 4 below.

Figure 20 - **Diagram 4: The problem of the nine dots**

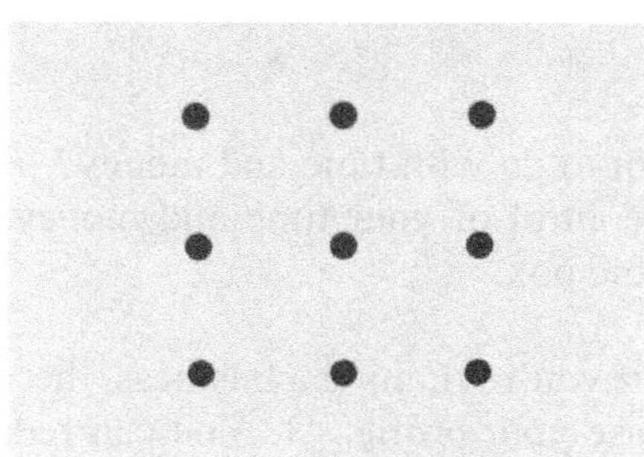

Try to solve the problem of connecting all nine dots by drawing just four straight lines connected end-to-end. Try it now, before you turn the page and see the solution.

Most people who see this problem for the first time need to draw at least five lines to connect all nine dots. They can't solve it in four because they think inside the box. They confine their thinking within an imaginary boundary drawn along the outside edge of the nine dots. To solve the problem you need to think outside the box. In fact, there *is* no box, just nine dots. Look at Diagram 5 for the solution.

Figure 21 - **Diagram 5: Solution to the problem of the nine dots**

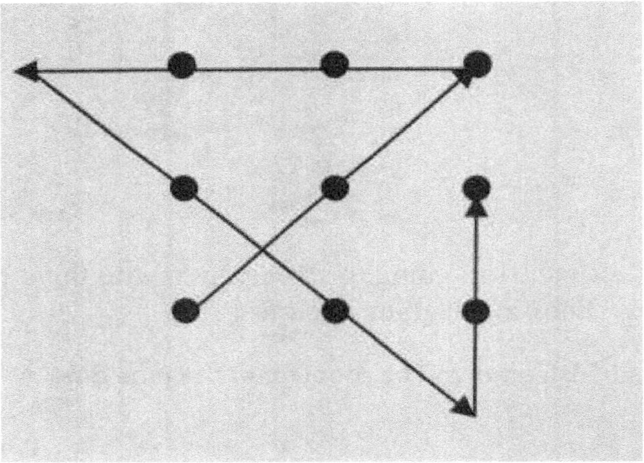

What's this got to do with time and money? *Heaps*. If you want to take control of your time and money, you have to think outside the box.

For example, if you're running a business, there are only two ways to increase your profits. 1. You can reduce expenses, or 2. You can increase income. Reducing expenses can only take you so far. If your annual expenses are ten thousand dollars, then even if you're able to reduce your expenses by 100%, the maximum improvement you can make to your bottom line is ten thousand dollars. But if you're able to increase your income, the sky's the limit. You can increase your income by ten, twenty, thirty thousand dollars or more if you have a good business plan. Reducing expenses is like thinking inside the box. Imagine your business as "the box." You have to look inside your business to identify ways to reduce expenses. You have to think inside the box. But to increase income you have to think *outside* the box, because that's where the money will come from. You won't find extra income looking *inside* the box. You have to look outside. You have to think outside the box.

Being *self-centred*, hoarding your time and money, jealously guarding what you've got, like the first general in the story at the beginning of the book, is like thinking *inside* the box. You can only go so far while you think inside the box. You're destined for *small change* in your life (pun intended).

On the other hand, being *self-less*, giving your time and money to the priority areas of your life and to others, is like thinking *outside* the box. The sky's the limit when you think outside the box. Big change only becomes possible when you think outside the box.

You'll never take control of your time and money without an attitude of giving. Without it, *they'll* always control *you*. If you want to take control of your time and money, first you have to get your priorities right. If you want to get your priorities right, you have to see the bigger picture and be willing to invest into it without always seeing immediate rewards. That requires a big heart, a generous spirit and a positive attitude. You have to be a cheerful giver. That requires you to think outside the box.

You have to give time and money to your family, your friends, your health and your hobbies. If you've been neglecting one or more of these areas up until now and you suddenly start giving back into it, don't be surprised if you don't reap immediate rewards. For a while, you just have to keep giving. You have to have faith that the rewards will come. And you have to be happy about it too, or you'll give up. You have to be a *cheerful* giver.

You can bank on it

Think of each priority area of your life - family, friends, health and hobbies - as having a bank account. When you give into that area of your life, you're topping up that account balance. When you suffer an ambush, or kick an own goal, you're withdrawing from that account. Even if you do nothing but neglect it, continuing the banking analogy, maintenance fees will erode your account balance.

If you continually withdraw from an account or neglect it for a long time, your account can become overdrawn. When that happens, everything you do seems to start going wrong. When you give, you don't feel any benefit. Even when you do nothing, you attract more fees and penalty interest. If you've overdrawn your account with your family, for instance, your deposits won't attract any "interest" until you get your account back into credit! You have to keep giving at those times, until your account gets back into credit, before you start to reap the rewards. And it's no use doing it with a snarl or a frown, because it won't be appreciated and you may as well not bother. You have to be a *cheerful* giver.

If your account is in credit, you get immediate rewards for additional giving. Even when you do nothing, you attract "interest"! Whatever you give is added to, or compounded, like compound interest on a bank account balance.

If you've identified your priorities and set goals to work on them, if you're monitoring your progress and making plans for continual improvement, if you're looking out for ambushes and avoiding own goals, you're a giving person already. You've demonstrated faith in yourself enough to see a bigger and better future. You've demonstrated faith in your family and friends enough to see a bigger and better future for your relationships with them.

It's in your own "interest"

In a sense, this is all just enlightened self-interest. You're really only giving to yourself because you see that investing in these areas of your life is in your own best interest. That's the whole tenor of this book, after all. It's just plain common sense to get your priorities right and live your life by them because that's the path to long-term health and happiness. To do anything else is shortsighted. In a sense, you're trading, not giving.

Selfless giving

To be truly successful in your giving, you have to rise above the notion of trading favours. If you give with an ulterior motive of getting some kickback, people will sense that and distrust you. You may as well not bother. But you don't want to give up. You want to reap the rewards of your giving.

The paradox of giving is that to *reap* a reward you have to give without *thought* of reward. It's an attitude thing. You can only get it by practising it. You can't sit in your chair and think yourself into it. It's like the chicken and the egg - which comes first, the *attitude* of giving or the *act* of giving? Logic says you can't truly give without first having the right attitude but the reality is you can't develop the right attitude without doing it. Practise makes perfect. Some things in life you just have to do to get good at them. If you have the faith to take the first step, your faith will be rewarded.

Only *selfless* giving will last. *Selfish* giving, or trading, won't last - you'll give up too soon if you don't see immediate benefits.

Insider trading

If you're putting yourself first all the time, you're thinking inside the box. You're an insider trader! Ebenezer Scrooge was an insider trader and it made his life miserable. In the financial world, insider trading is a crime that people go to jail for. You need to think outside the box. You need to become an "outsider trader".

This applies to time as well as money. Many a time I've been miserable in myself and have declined an invitation to go out somewhere. The result is that I remain miserable. However, I've learned that nine times out of ten it is better to accept and go out than to stay at home, because when I'm out I usually forget myself and my own woes as I become immersed in other things and other people. I've concluded that the reason for this is:

The problem is usually where you are,
not where you're going.

In other words, the solution is outside the box!

Common Cents

Giving is more fun than receiving

Do you know that giving can be more fun than receiving? Receiving gifts at Christmas time is satisfying if you get what you want but it can be disappointing if you don't. I find I often get more fun finding the perfect present for someone else and watching them open it, than I get opening my own presents.

If you learn to give without thought of reward, you'll *always* be satisfied and that is reward in itself. Learn to give for the joy of giving. Learn to be a cheerful giver. You learn by doing.

A true test of your giving attitude is to give to someone or something else that can't possibly benefit you. You have to do it anonymously too, because if someone finds out, you risk being rewarded, and that would be trading, not giving.

If you want to be a great person, learn to give. Think of anyone you greatly admire. People are remembered and admired for what they have given, not for what they have received.

You reap what you sow

A farmer has seed for sowing and seed for food. Some of his seed is to provide food for his table and the rest is for next year's crop. If the farmer eats all his seed in one year, he and his family will be fat for one year but they'll have nothing to sow for next year's crop. They'll be hungry the rest of their lives. When giving becomes second nature to you, you'll see that some of all you have is for your immediate use or consumption, some is for you to invest in the priority areas of your life and some can be scattered abroad (given away) [22].

If you want something, you have to give it away!

You reap what you sow. What goes around comes around. If you want cornstalks, you have to plant corn seeds. If you want friends, you have to be a friend (chapter one). If you want to be forgiven, you have to forgive others (chapter seven). If you want more time, you have to invest time in the priority areas of your life (chapter one). If you want more money, you have to be generous. Money's made round to go round.

The expanding universe vs the black hole

Scientists say our universe is constantly *expanding*, spiraling outwards from some theoretical point of origin. It's as if God picked up all the stars one day and flung them out in all directions. Scientists also say there are parts of our universe

---

[22] This message, indeed much of this chapter, is encapsulated in 2nd Corinthians 9:6-7 *"He who sows sparingly will also reap sparingly, and he who sows bountifully will also reap bountifully. So let each one give as he purposes in his heart, not grudgingly or of necessity; for God loves a cheerful giver."*

that are constantly *contracting*. They call these black holes. Black holes are tiny points in space where large amounts of mass have accumulated and they exert such a strong gravitational pull that anything coming near them is sucked in and can't escape. Even light itself is sucked in and can't escape, which is why black holes are black.

When you practise selfless giving, you don't consciously give to get. But you *do* get something back. What you *get* is a greater capacity to *give!* In a very real sense, your world becomes bigger and bigger as your focus broadens and your heart opens up, like our expanding universe. It's a never-ending spiral upwards and outwards. There's always more.

The opposite is true when you practise self-centredness. Your world becomes smaller and smaller as your thinking and activities become more and more inwardly focused and weigh more and more heavily on you. You slowly recede into a tiny black hole where no one can see into and *you* can't see out of.

How to defy common sense

Successful time and money management isn't rocket science. This book is all about common sense ways to manage your time and money. But this chapter about selfless giving seems to *defy* common sense. Maybe it does, but the fact is that it works, and in my life it is the single most important principle of all. I started to learn the principle twenty-two years ago. I had always resented giving money away up until then. To me, ten cents given away was ten cents wasted. I figured that I earned it so I should keep it. Twenty-two years ago, I was reading about the principle of selfless giving and decided to test it out. I prepared my family budget to see how much I could afford to give to this experiment. I concluded that my *outgoings* exceeded my *incomings* and my *upkeep* was going to be my *downfall.* I had obviously *never* had enough money to live on and had no right to be here! Have you ever done a budget and found out you couldn't exist? Like a true fanatic, (see chapter seven) I pressed on regardless with my plan. It then took me another six months to find my wallet but eventually one day I gave away twenty dollars. I did this each week for eight weeks and an amazing thing happened: It made no difference at all to my bank account. Before the experiment, I had no money in the bank. After the experiment, I still had no money in the bank. I was no worse off. That's when I came up with the idea of Parkinson's Law of Money Management introduced in chapter four - *Expenditure expands to consume the available income.* I was intrigued, so after eight weeks I increased my giving dramatically. You can guess what happened: Nothing. That's actually understating the truth. In fact, I seemed to have *more* money in my bank account. I've had less financial worries ever since. I never have *lots* of money, but I never did. More importantly, I always have what I need and I have something else that's far more valuable - *peace of mind.* Going on holiday to finish writing this book is a classic example. I mentioned it in chapter six. Within 24 hours of making the call to book my holiday, money came from an unexpected source that was exactly the amount I needed to pay for my holiday. Financial miracles like that happen to me all the time now, ever since I started to practise selfless giving.

How to experience a financial miracle

The only times I have financial difficulty are those rare moments when I step out of selflessness and into self-centredness. The moment I step back into selflessness, my financial problems miraculously go away. You can call it luck, you can call it an interesting psychological phenomenon, you can call it karma, you can call it yin and yang, or you can call it a law of the universe, like gravity or $E=mc^2$. But *none* of those things offer a rational explanation for my financial miracles; they're only excuses to stop thinking about it; and they require too much blind faith for me to take them seriously. The only *rational* explanation I can think of is that there *is* a real, omniscient, omnipotent and omnipresent God, and that He takes a personal interest in my affairs. My financial miracles are no coincidences, they're God incidences. The prophet Malachi says in the Bible that if we honour God with our finances, then God will protect our finances and bless our finances [23]. Honouring God with my finances means giving generously and it means being honest and open in all my financial dealings. When I honour God with my finances, my bank balance is healthy. When I forget to honour God with my finances, I find myself in financial difficulty. So what Malachi says is true in my experience. Regardless of how hard it may be for some people to accept, it's the only rational explanation I've heard for my financial miracles.

If you think you can't afford to give,
then you can't afford not to!

Remember when I prepared my budget to see how generous I could *afford* to be? Don't do that. It didn't work for me either. If you give what you think you can afford to give, if you give what you don't need, that's not selfless giving. That's just *waste disposal*. Don't wait until you're rich to start giving. If you can't give ten dollars, you'll never give a

[23] Malachi 3:10-11

million. Don't think you can't afford to give. When you realise the benefits, you can't afford not to!

Give what's right, not what's left

In chapter four, I introduced a goal of saving ten percent of your income. Paying yourself, that is. Why not set a goal to *give* ten percent. If you can't come at that, start small and increase gradually. Start by saving one percent and giving one percent - two percent in total. Don't think you can't afford it. If your income is low, one percent isn't much anyway. If your weekly income is only a hundred dollars, one percent is just a dollar. If you make a thousand, one percent is just ten dollars. Remember what Einstein said – everything is relative!

Be prepared

Don't give anything you're not prepared to lose, otherwise your resentment will show and it will sour the gift and make it worthless. Give without thought of reward. Give for the joy of giving. Be a *cheerful* giver.

Don't *lend* anything you're not prepared to lose, either. When you lend things - time, money, or possessions - you risk not getting them back. Be prepared for that. Sure, you *want* it returned, but if you can't cope with its loss, you're setting yourself up for disappointment by lending it. Don't lend your car to your teenager, for example, if you're not prepared for the car to get damaged.
To be fair, *don't borrow anything you're not prepared to pay for* if it's lost or broken.

The greatest gift you can give is your love and concern for other people - family, friends, business associates, and even total strangers. It costs nothing and offers high return on investment. You have to *invest* in relationships, because:

People don't care how much you know
until they know how much you care

Two of the most important gifts I gave my children when they were aged between about five and eleven were a sense of *obedience* and *respect.* We had a successful formula for discipline. First, I'd give a quick, light slap or tap on the hand to arrest their behaviour and nip it in the bud. Then, I'd ask them what they did wrong and they'd have to admit it and explain it in their own words. Then they'd say, "I'm sorry, please forgive me, I won't do it again." Then I'd say, "I forgive you" and give them a hug. I reserved more severe punishment for repeated or deliberate disobedience. Lying and rebellion were the worst, because they were so deliberate.

At first, I had to discipline *myself* to discipline my children. It's tempting for a parent to let things go, but that's false economy. If you hold onto things, discipline loses its effectiveness. Sooner or later, you're going to blow your top and it will be about some little thing - the proverbial straw that breaks the camel's back. Your response will be seen in the light of that one little thing, not the twenty that went unpunished before it. You'll be seen as inconsistent, unstable, and quite unfair. They won't learn a thing from it, because they won't understand it, and they'll resent you.

Discipline has to be swift to be effective [24]. And it must always be done out of love, never anger or revenge.

From about the age of twelve upwards, I found the most important gift to my children is to keep open the channels of *communication.* I still teach them at this age about obedience and respect but I'm cautious not to hound them, not to nag them when they don't clean their room, not to get too worried about what they wear or how they do their hair. The most important thing is to keep talking, because as they grow older and become more independent I'll have less control and less say in their lives. If I cut myself off now, I'll have *no* say in future and they won't come to me when they have *real* problems, for fear of rebuke or ridicule. I have to consider my priorities constantly - what's more important, a tidy room or open communications?

I have to risk letting them grow up

I don't treat them as children any more. I have to risk letting them grow up. In the Biblical tradition, a child becomes an adult at the age of thirteen. That seems far-fetched to our modern society, but in former times a thirteen-year-old had the strength and maturity to do an adult's work and was required to do it. There was no social class of "teenagers" – that only developed more recently. So I think of my teenagers as adults [25]. Of course, there still have to be boundaries and standards of behaviour, as there are for adults. We spell them out clearly and write them down if necessary. For instance,

---

[24] Ecclesiastes 8:11 *"Because the sentence against an evil work is not executed speedily, therefore the heart of the sons of men is fully set in them to do evil."*

[25] My teenagers have since grown up and become adults of impressive maturity and integrity. We must have done something right.

they can keep their own room untidy, but not common areas. There's a balance between freedom and responsibility. Also, there's a difference between a clean room and a tidy room. Untidy is ok but unclean is not!

If you lend your car to your teenager, expect the best and be prepared for the worst. Consider your priorities - what's more important, the car or your relationship? If the car gets damaged, don't blow it, don't kick an own goal by giving in to the temptation to lose your temper and make an almighty scene. Don't lose control. *Take control.* Let your first response be *gratitude* that they are alive to tell you about it. Then, tell them you forgive them and tell them you love them. When everyone has calmed down, calmly state the repercussions, such as grounding, and the terms of restoration, such as working off the cost of the repairs.

The Sandwich method

I like the Toastmasters formula (also known as the *sandwich* method) - *start* with a positive affirmation or compliment, *follow* with the bad news or a constructive criticism and *end* with another positive.

When you have the opportunity and the privilege of speaking into someone's life, whether at home, at work, or anywhere else, avoid *negative* reinforcement. Instead, use *positive* reinforcement. Negative reinforcement only entrenches the *undesired* behaviour in the hearer's mind. Positive reinforcement places a *can-do* message in the hearer's mind. Examples of the wrong way to talk and the right way are in the table (Table 2) that follows.

Figure 22 - **Table 2: Positive vs negative reinforcement**

Negative reinforcement	**Positive reinforcement**
message spoken: *You don't help me* message received: *I don't help you*	message spoken: *Please help me* message received: *You want me to help you*
message spoken: *You never help me* message received: *I never help you*	message spoken: *I need your help* message received: *You need my help*
message spoken: *You won't help me* message received: *I won't help you*	message spoken: *You can help me* message received: *I can help you*
message spoken: *You can't help me, can you?* message received: *No, I can't help you*	message spoken: *You can help me, can't you?* message received: *Yes, I can help you*
message spoken: *You wouldn't help me, would you?* message received: *No, I wouldn't help you*	message spoken: *You would help me, wouldn't you?* message received: *Yes, I would help you*
message spoken: *You always fail* message received: *I always fail, so I won't try*	message spoken: *You can do this* message received: *I can do this*

Common Cents

Here's my final thought on giving:

When others are suffering,
your gifts mean so much more to them.

Continuing the financial analogy, think of it as buying into a depressed market. When expectations are lowest, return on investment is highest, if you invest in good stocks. And your family come from the best stock, don't they!

1. Start thinking outside the box
2. Give without thought of reward
3. Give for the joy of giving
4. Giving is more fun than receiving
5. Be a cheerful giver
6. Be a selfless giver
7. It's in your own "interest"
8. You learn by doing
9. You reap what you sow
10. If you want something, you have to give it away
11. When you don't give to get, what you get is a greater capacity to give
12. You can't afford *not* to be generous
13. Don't lend anything you're not prepared to lose
14. Don't borrow anything you're not prepared to pay for

15. People don't care how much you know until they know how much you care
16. Speak words of positive reinforcement
17. Buy into depressed markets
18. Start and end on a positive note

Chapter 10 - Make up your mind

"I used to be indecisive... but now I'm not so sure"

"I thought I was wrong once... but I was mistaken"

Seriously, indecision and poor decision-making, planning and problem solving are among the worst wasters of time and money.

If you're indecisive, slow to make decisions, or just plain incapable of making a decision, you can waver and procrastinate over something for hours, days, weeks, months, even years and never do anything about it. Maybe you're like Pa Kettle. Pa originally featured in the comedy movie, *The Egg and I*, which was the spin off for the *Ma and Pa Kettle* series of movies. Pa put everything off. His favourite saying was, and you have to say it in a long drawl to get the original torpor, *"I'll get around to that... one of these days."* One of these days never comes.

At the other extreme, if you're impulsive and make flippant decisions without weighing the pros and cons appropriately, you can get yourself into a lot of hot water and waste a lot of time and money trying to extricate yourself.

Good decision-making is an essential tool to help you take control of your time and money.

Here's a six-step process to help you make up your mind. Most decisions won't require all six stages.

1. Test your options against your goals and values
2. Which moves you closer to your goals?
3. Draw a mind map
4. Get a second opinion
5. Let peace rule
6. The cooling off period

A word of warning: Never make important decisions when you're sick or down in the dumps. Your thinking gets clouded and you naturally feel bad about everything. It's senseless to make important decisions under those conditions.

Now let's look at each step in detail...

Step 1 - Test your options against your goals and values

The first step in good decision-making is to test your options against your goals and values.

By now, you need to have worked these out, written them down and pinned them on the wall or somewhere else where you'll see them every day. Paste a copy in your diary. If you haven't finished this activity yet, buzz back and complete Worksheet 2 (your goals) in chapter two and Worksheet 13 (your values) in chapter seven. You might have updated your goals or values in chapter six, so make sure you're using the right version.

A good decision will never conflict with your values and will never set you back in your goals. Immediately discard any options that do.

Step 2 - Which moves you closer to your goals?

When you have to decide between two or more courses of action that are *all* good choices, that are *all* consistent with your goals and values, that *all* pass step number one, then you decide by choosing which one moves you *closest* to your goals. Which one provides the most "bang for your buck"?

Step 3 - Draw a mind map

What do you do if you have two or more good choices and can't pick a winner? Or what if your decision doesn't affect your goals and values? Or what if you have *no* options, for instance you have a problem but no idea how to solve it?

You could start by having a brainstorming session and making a list of everything you know about the subject you have in mind, but there is a better way. It's called a *mind map*. Making a list is a linear way of processing your thoughts. It limits your creativity and efficiency because it's awkward when you want to change, reorder, or add sub-points to your list. A mind map gives you more flexibility to go off on tangents and come back to your main thought process. A mind map helps you work the way your mind naturally works, that is, *randomly*.

I started this chapter with the title and nothing else. I couldn't decide how to start it, what to put in it or how to end it, so I drew a mind map. I wrote down all my thoughts and developed each one as fully as I could. Then I prioritised them and, *voilà*, within half an hour I had the contents and structure figured out! The next diagram (Diagram 6) shows my original mind map. It's crude and messy and you can't read much of it because of the bad writing and the size reduction from a full A4 page. I could have rewritten it but I thought it better to show you the original to prove it doesn't have to be a work of art to be effective and not every stroke has to be perfect.

Figure 23 - **Diagram 6: The author's mind map**

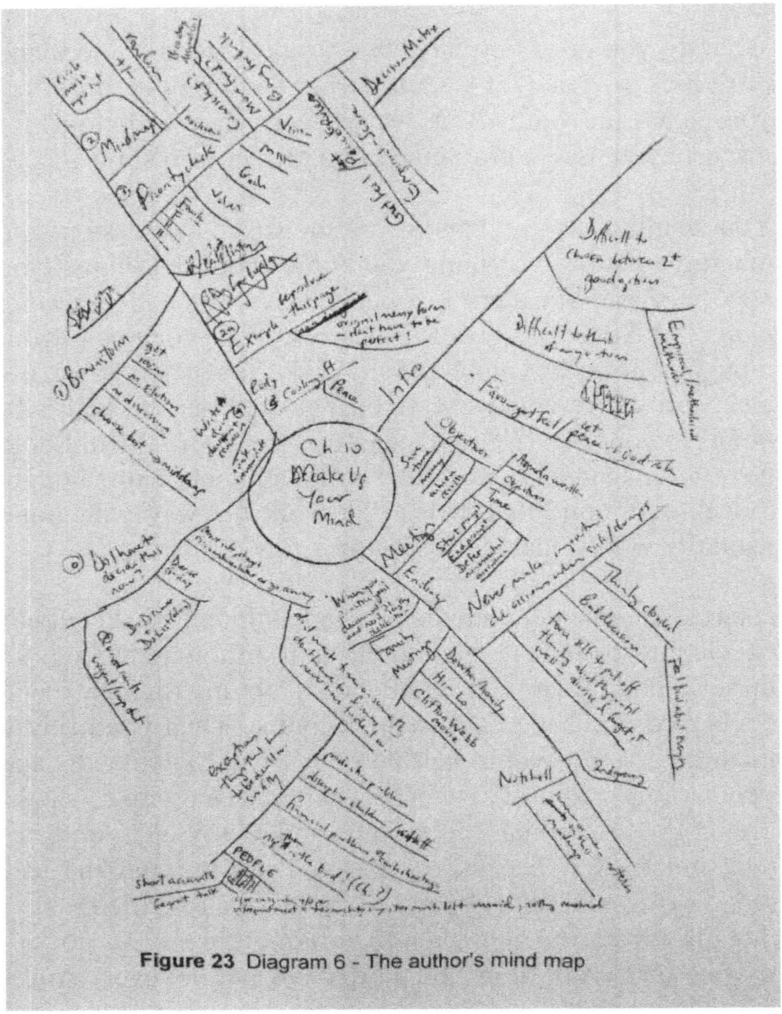

Figure 23 Diagram 6 - The author's mind map

Next, I describe the process of drawing your own mind map. As you follow the process, you can look back at the diagram and see how I did it.

You start your mind map by writing your problem statement in the middle of a blank page and circling it. Call this the trunk. This is the trunk of your thought tree, from which all your thoughts are going to sprout. Then you draw branches radiating from the trunk (you have to imagine you're looking down on the tree from above). Each branch represents a major aspect of the problem or one of several options you're considering to solve it. You write the description of each branch along its length. Then you draw twigs off the branches to represent sub-aspects or sub-options. Again, you write the description of each twig along its length. You can then draw twigs off other twigs and so on, if you wish. You don't have to develop all the branches before starting on the twigs. You develop the map in whatever order your mind takes you. At the end of it, you've captured all the information you have on the subject and hopefully you've identified all your options.

When I'm using a mind map to make a decision, I often write a "+" on one side of each branch and a "-" on the other. Then I draw twigs for all the pros of each branch down its "+" side and all the cons down its "-" side. If one side of the branch is weightier than the other, the picture often tells the story.

Another technique is to take a highlighter pen and highlight the most critical twigs on your mind map. The picture tells the story and "highlights" which way to go.

Hopefully now your options are clearer and you can take them through steps one and two above to arrive at your decision.

Step 4 - Get a second opinion

By now, you've made up your mind. Sometimes, as Solomon wrote in the Book of Proverbs, there is safety in a multitude of counselors [26]. Run your decision past someone whose opinion you value and trust.

If you need to schedule a meeting with a group of people, take a few tips for planning effective meetings…

1. Prepare a written agenda, clear objectives, and a time frame.
2. Invite the key people you want to come to your meeting. Provide them beforehand with copies of your agenda and your objectives, and inform them of the allotted time frame. They'll appreciate that, because on important or difficult issues it's wise to weigh a matter and let the dust settle in your mind before arriving at a conclusion. It would be unfair and unwise to expect your guests to come to a meeting cold and expect an instant decision. Provide them with as much background information as you can. Discuss it with them individually before the meeting. When you do this, people can come to your meeting prepared to finalise the issues, not just to find out what they are. Then you stand a chance of achieving your objectives and avoiding more meetings.

[26] Proverbs 11:14 *"Where there is no counsel, the people fall; But in the multitude of counsellors there is safety."*, 15:22 *"Without counsel, plans go awry, But in the multitude of counsellors they are established."* and 24:6 *"For by wise counsel you will wage your own war, And in a multitude of counsellors there is safety."*

3. Start the meeting on time, defer all non-essential discussion, and finish on time. They'll love you for that.

Step 5 - Let peace rule

When you make a good decision, you should feel at peace about it. If you don't feel at peace about your decision, you've probably missed something and need to run through the first four decision-making steps again.

Step 6 - The cooling off period

Some decisions you have to implement immediately. Decisions that involve other people, and other urgent matters such as a cash flow crisis, you have to deal with immediately. People problems are always urgent because people's perception of a problem changes with time in random ways you can't predict, so it's nearly always best to nip them in the bud.

If your decision can wait, allow yourself a cooling off period. Priorities may change or more information may come to light. Write down your decision, the reasons for it, and the date. Attach your mind map if you made one. Choose a review date in a week's or a month's time, write it in your diary and put the paperwork away until then. When the day comes, if you still feel at peace about the decision, do it!

I have a bad habit of second-guessing my decisions. Call it last-minute jitters. Whenever I make an important decision, even after following the six steps, the moment I take the first step to implement it, I start to doubt. I've learned to ignore this impulse and to press on, but it's never easy. Have the strength of your convictions. When you've done the right thing and made a good decision, don't hesitate to implement it. Don't change the decision because of mere doubt. Have faith in the decision making process. If the orders are signed and sealed, deliver them! Don't be tempted to change horses in midstream.

1. Test your options against your goals and values
2. Which moves you closer to your goals?
3. Draw a mind map
4. Get a second opinion
5. Let peace rule
6. The cooling off period

Above all:

- Don't second-guess a good decision
- Never make important decisions when you're sick or down in the dumps

Tips for effective meetings:

- Have a written agenda, objectives and timeframe
- Come prepared to finalise the issues, not to find out what they are
- Start on time, defer all non-essentials, finish on time

The Final Word

The content of this book isn't drawn from theory. It's based on what works for me. Just about everything written was learned from the (often bitter) firsthand experience of getting it wrong, finding out what works, and then getting it right. I think that's a good basis from which to write this book. I'm not telling you what to do; I'm sharing what works for me. You can decide whether and how to apply it for yourself.

Common sense should tell you that what I'm writing is sound and good. But there *is* another source to back it up. Many things experienced and written in this book have a foundation or parallel in the Bible. I didn't *learn* all these lessons from it and I didn't preach them to you from it, but many times when I learned a new lesson in life, I found out later on that I'd stumbled onto yet another scriptural principle. If I looked there first, I could have saved a lot of time and money. But I had to learn the hard way.

For instance, Jesus started public ministry at the age of thirty and ended it three years later. Which means that in preparation for just three years of effective service, He spent a whole thirty years doing… *what?* In answer, there's just one sentence that describes how He spent his early adult life, between the ages of thirteen and thirty. It's at the end of Luke chapter two. A Doctor by profession, Luke chose his words carefully and precisely. The good Doctor Luke says that all those years, Jesus *"increased in wisdom and stature, and in favour with God and men."* [27] That's all he says. In other words, He was getting His priorities right, patiently and

---

[27] Luke 2:52 *"And Jesus increased in wisdom and stature, and in favor with God and men."*

faithfully building a strong foundation for a well-balanced life. He was developing his mind, developing his physical strength and cultivating his relationships. As a carpenter, he was learning and plying a healthy, useful trade. That's chapter one of my book!

What better could we do than follow *His* example?

Appendix 1 - Preparing a budget

I'm going to use the example of a typical family budget to demonstrate some basic principles that apply to all budgets.

There are many different ways to prepare a budget. I found this one works for me. Whether you use this method or another, the important thing is to have one! The hardest thing about a budget is the blank piece of paper you start with the first time. Don't worry if your first one isn't accurate. No budget is. Just start somewhere and keep refining it as you go. You might find my simple two step method a good and easy way to start, because it doesn't go into a lot of detail and it doesn't depend on technology.

Step 1 - Estimate your annual income and expenditure

By referring to your cheque butts, credit card statements, payslips, tax returns, and whatever other documentation you have, prepare the following lists. You can use the worksheet (Worksheet 16) that follows.

1. Weekly income, eg wages
2. Fortnightly income, eg social security
3. Monthly income
4. Annual or other income
5. Weekly expenses, eg savings, cash for food & groceries etc (on average)
6. Fortnightly expenses
7. Monthly expenses, eg rent, mortgage and loan repayments, health and other insurance premiums, credit card payments, bank fees
8. Annual or other expenses, eg car rego, insurance, CTP, council and water rates, school fees, gas, electricity, phone, home insurance

Add the annual totals of the first four lists. This is your total annual incomings. Now add the annual totals of the next four lists. This is your total annual outgoings. If your outgoings exceed your incomings, your upkeep is going to be your downfall and you need to make changes.

Preparing these lists is a one-time exercise. Every month, however, you should glance at the lists to make sure they are up-to-date.

Figure 24 - **Worksheet 16: Budgeted income and expenditure**

List	Description	Amount	$ p.a.
Weekly income			
Fortnightly income			
Monthly income			
Other income			
TOTAL	**Total Income**		
Weekly Expense			
Fortnightly Expense			
Monthly Expense			
Other Expense			
TOTAL	**Total Expenses**		
BALANCE	**Income Less Expenses**		

Step 2 - Monitor your cash flow

At the start of every month, draw up a cash flow forecast for the next 1-3 months, like the example that follows (Table 3).

The further ahead you plan, the less surprises you'll get. It's little use finding out just a week ahead of time that you're going to run short of cash. Better to know further ahead of time so you can plan around it. On the other hand, the further ahead you plan, the more your plan will change. That's why I suggest one month as a minimum and three as a maximum for most people.

I've designed this system so anybody can do it with pencil and paper. If you want to get more sophisticated, you can use a computer program such as Quicken®. I hesitate to suggest using a computer spreadsheet program because of the risk of miscalculating your running daily balance, which is the most critical element of the plan. If you're using a spreadsheet, be aware when adding or deleting rows that the formulas in the cells directly above and below the insertion or deletion point will require repair. If you don't know what I'm talking about, don't use a spreadsheet!

The example provided below in Table 3 forecasts a cash flow shortage in the first week of the month. You could plan around this problem a number of ways, eg by paying $750 off the credit card on the due date and the remaining $50 the following week, or paying the car rego by credit card to even-out your cash flow. If it wasn't so long before the next payday, you could also plan around the problem by postponing the weekly shopping by a day.

Figure 25 - **Table 3: Budgeted cash flow example**

Date	Description	Amount	Balance	Comment
	Opening balance		820	
1	Bank fees	-20	800	
2	Wages	+550	1350	
	Transfer to Savings account	-80	1270	
3	Cash withdrawal	-200	1070	
4	Credit card balance due	-800	270	
5	Car rego due	-300	-30	overdrawn
9	Wages	+550	520	
	Transfer to Savings account	-80	440	
10	Cash withdrawal	-200	240	
11	Social Security	+100	340	
16	Wages	+550	890	
	Transfer to Savings account	-80	810	
17	Cash withdrawal	-200	610	
23	Wages	+550	1160	
	Transfer to Savings account	-80	1080	
24	Cash withdrawal	-200	880	
25	Social Security	+100	980	
26	House & car insurance	-100	880	

Doing this every month has two important benefits:

1. You will see any cash flow shortages in advance and can plan around them.

2. If you have no cash flow shortages, maybe you can free up some cash and avoid it sitting there doing nothing, by transferring it to savings or paying off some debt.

The best-laid plans of mice and men

I remember Arthur Dent chatting with a hyper-intelligent pan-dimensional mouse in *Hitchhiker's Guide to the Galaxy.* Arthur makes an offhand remark about "the best-laid plans of mice and men." The bemused mouse replies, "What have men got to do with it?" because in his reality, mice make all the plans and men are just dumb "lab rats." My point is that, *whether you're a man or a mouse*, your best-laid plans will suffer change.

Whenever an unplanned change happens to your budget (for example, you have to withdraw extra cash for an emergency), you write the change on the cash flow worksheet and enter the *cumulative* value of all the changes in a *Change* column. The purpose of the Change column is to save you having to update all the running balances. If you're using a computer program, it will automatically recalculate all the balances, so you don't need a Change column. This is the main advantage of using a computer.

For example, let's say you have to withdraw an extra $50 in the second week and again the following week. The Worksheet now looks like Table 4, with the changes in italics. If there are no other changes during the month, the account balance at the end of the month will be $100 less, i.e. $780, not $880 as originally forecast.

You can copy and use the blank cash flow worksheet (Worksheet 17) at the end of the appendix for your own budget. Don't forget to leave yourself plenty of blank lines for changes and additions. Happy budgeting!

Figure 26 - **Table 4: Budgeted cash flow example with changes**

Date	Description	Amount	Balance	Change	Comment
	Opening balance		820		
1	Bank fees	-20	800		
2	Wages	+550	1350		
	Transfer to Savings	-80	1270		
3	Cash withdrawal	-200	1070		
4	Credit card balance	-800	270		
5	Car rego due	-300	-30		overdrawn
9	Wages	+550	520		
	Transfer to Savings	-80	440		
10	Cash withdrawal	*-250*	240	*-50*	
11	Social Security	+100	340		
16	Wages	+550	890		
	Transfer to Savings	-80	810		
17	Cash withdrawal	-200	610		
18	*Additional cash needed*	*-50*		*-100*	
23	Wages	+550	1160		
	Transfer to Savings	-80	1080		
24	Cash withdrawal	-200	880		
25	Social Security	+100	980		
26	House & car insurance	-100	880		

Figure 27 - **Worksheet 17: Budgeted cash flow blank worksheet**

Budgeted cash flow

Month: ______________ Opening balance $ ___________

Date	Description	Amount	Balance	Change	Comment

Further reading and resources

Books:

The Five Love Languages of Teenagers by Gary Chapman

The One Minute Manager by Blanchard & Johnson

In Search of Excellence by Peters & Waterman

The Oxford Dictionary of Quotations

Bible quotations in this book, unless otherwise specified, are from The Holy Bible, New King James Version,

Web resources:

www.achieversgroup.com.au

www.biblegateway.com

www.christianityworks.com

www.dgreen.id.au

www.freemansfitness.com.au

www.juliefreemancoaching.com.au

www.juliegreenart.com

www.prioritymanagement.com

Index

Other books by the author

Toast

A story about fighting the Berowra bushfires and coping with post-traumatic stress.

First Printed in Australia in 2003
A5 paperback, 128pp
International and eBook version published in 2015

How to get Common Cents

To get **Common Cents**, or to order **Toast**, and to see other works by the author, visit David Green's Amazon page www.amazon.com/author/green or his personal website www.dgreen.id.au.

Notes

Made in the USA
Monee, IL
04 November 2026

67383954R00115